The Spirit's Pathway Traced

DID IT PRE-EXIST AND DOES IT REINCARNATE AGAIN INTO MORTAL LIFE?

By

J. M. PEEBLES, M. D., M. A.

——*Author of*——

"Seers of the Ages." "Three Journeys Around the World." "Immortality and Our Future Homes." "Obsession, or the Reign of Evil Spirits." "The Christ Question Settled." "Discussion on Reincarnation." "Death Defeated, or the Psychic Secret of How to Keep Young." The Victoria Institute's Rejected Address, "Vaccination a Curse." "Spiritualism vs. Materialism." And other Books and Pamphlets.

The world is my parish—and Truth my authority. One origin, one brotherhood, and one final destiny for all humanity.

PUBLISHED BY

DR. PEEBLES INSTITUTE OF HEALTH

BATTLE CREEK. MICH.

CONTENTS.

5

6 CONTENTS.

WHY THIS BOOK?

"Books are man's worlds—his great attempts to speak
  The meaning of the oracle within;
And worlds are God's books, in which he writes
A memoir of Himself in love to man."

The question 'Why this Book?' is natural, considering the numerous writers and the crowded libraries of the country.

"It may seem strange," said the quaint Walt Whitman, "that the utmost growth of a nation is its own born literature, either prose or poetry." These are the flower and the fruitage of any rising cycle of time. In no civilization does the most advanced science remain true for centuries. Chemistry, with its seventeen elements, in my academic days seventy years ago, is now but a vanished memory. Archimedes and Euclid are barely mentioned today, while Homer and Virgil delight the modern student as they did the Greek and Roman heroes of old.

When the inspiration came to me some two years ago like "a mighty rushing wind" to write "The Demonism of the Ages and of Spirit Obsessions," I hesitated, saying in the silence, is it wanted? Would it be welcomed? Would it benefit investigators, especially those who sit doubtingly, hopingly, by that shrine of mystery—the Invisible?

Pondering, the voice said in tenderest tones of earnestness,—"Write—Write! *The time has come.*" And like Paul, I, before some unseen spiritual Agrippa, "was not disobedient to the heavenly vision."

7

The book was launched, and the canonading crash of criticism came, exceedingly noisy and tremendously terrific for a time. The class of Spiritualists who believe death to be the great deliverer, if not the savior of the world, pronounced it "the worst book ever written except the Bible;" another wrote that "the author ought to be imprisoned;" another wrote that "both him and the book should be burned in effigy;" another wrote in the "Light of Truth" that the writer "ought to be impaled on some grinning devil's red-hot pitchfork and thrust into a boiling cauldron;" and still another, seeing by the press that I was about to sail for England, "hoped to heaven, that the steamer that carried Peebles would go down with him and all his devils."

These little eddying ripples upon the river of time, soon proved to be but "spent forces" increasing the calls for the book, giving place to the calm words of the great seer, Dr. A. J. Davis, W. T. Stead, of the London *Review of Reviews,* Prof. E. Whipple, Pres. Moses Hull, editors of the *Progressive Thinker* and the *Banner of Light,* the *Balance,* the *Arena,* the *Literary Digest,* &c. which may be briefly summed up—"This book was needed." "It will be a chart to the investigators?" "It was wanted." "It will cause care in the seances," "prove a light-house of warning," and other commendations from those who live in a realm above all envies and petty jealousies; while J. R. Francis, whom I have personally known these forty years, and known to esteem and honor, said in his weekly "Thinker," "*Such a timely book would make any man immortal!*" A fourth edition revised will be issued early this autumn.

Well—several months ago the voice came again—
"*Write—Write—the time has come!*"

As before, I hesitated, saying, is such a book as I
seem to see in vision, wanted? Will it not be disap-
pointing? Will it not call out harsh, and probably
vicious criticism? Is there a demand for a book dealing more with the ideal and the metaphysical than with
the objective phenomenal—"Write!" again said the
voice.

Obeying, the writer has to say that his sole object
in this discursive volume has been to arouse a thoughtful mood, hoping to bring into conscious activity the
higher spiritual forces of the inner nature.

Certain persons who have not thought along the
line of the spirit's origin may think that the theories
of pre-existence and return into human bodies for special purposes, irrational and iconoclastic; but if they
clearly comprehend the author's purpose they will
see that his aim has been to present tentatively the
higher teachings of life and immortality in relation to
involution and evolution—cause and effect in their
relational continuity, demonstrating for all a glorious
eternity of unfoldment.

"Speak thy thought if thou believ'st it;
  Let it jostle whom it may,
E'en altho the unwise scorn it,
  Or the obstinate gainsay;
Every seed that grows tomorrow
  Lies beneath a clod today.

"If our sires (the noble-hearted
  Pioneers of things to come),
Had like some been weak and timid,
  Traitors to themselves, and dumb,
Where would be our present knowledge?
Where the hoped Milennium?"

INTRODUCTION.

"And as to your Life I reckon you are the leavings of
    many deaths,
(No doubt I have died myself ten thousand times be-
    fore)."

"My foothold is tenon'd and mortis'd in granite,
    I laugh at what you call dissolution, and I know the
    amplitude of time."

—Walt Whitman.

Many years ago, *as we count time,* through the
courtesy of a mutual friend, I had the honor of an
afternoon with Emerson in his Concord library, and
upon leaving had the further pleasure of bearing a
note from him to Walt Whitman, then in the city of
Washington.

Previously I had felt the tender touch of Whitman's spirit when Eliza W. Farnham, a noted writer,
author of "The Ideal Attained," and at this time Ma-
tron of the Woman's Department in a California
Institution for the insane.

At the close of a series of lectures delivered in the
City Hall, Stockton, in 1861, upon both the intuitive
and phenomenal proofs of a future existence with the
corollary, a converse between the worlds visible and
invisible, I was introduced to Mrs. Farnham, already
a believer in angel ministries, and who invited me to
call upon her. So doing, she read to me on several
evenings extracts from Whitman's "Leaves of Grass."
They were then new to me. She was a splendid reader,
and her annotations upon some of the passages were
comparable to richest aromas from a truly spiritual

genius. Listening to her readings and her clear, uplifting comments upon them, I was thrilled to my being's core. Understanding, she could interpret him.
She knew how to elucidate his dark lines of mystery
called poems—poems unique, beautiful, inspiring, yet
devoid of rhyme or rhythmic measure. Who could read
his lines—"The Song of The Open Road," without
being led, charmed along to the border realm of ecstasy?

Here follow sentences and passages selected almost
at random from his scattered leaves:

"The song is to the singer and comes back most to him;
 The teaching is to the teacher, and comes back most
  to him."

This poet of nature, like nearly all inspired poets,
believed in the human spirit's pre-existence. Yet, like
the philosopher, A. Bronson Alcott, he did not seek to
force this great truth upon those whom he esteemed
unprepared to receive it, nevertheless it runs like
golden threads through his prose and verse.

"I see, Hermes unsuspected, dying, well-beloved, saying
 To the people, 'do not weep for me.'
 This is not my true country. I have lived banished
  from my true country—I now go back there.
 I go to that celestial sphere, where every one goes in
  his turn."

"Let me glide noiselessly forth:
 With the key of softness unlock the door—
 With a whisper, set ope the door, O Soul!"
"I know that the hand of God is the promise of my
  own;
 I know that the spirit of God is the brother of my own;
 And that all the men ever born are also my brothers,
  and the women my sisters and lovers,
 And that a kelson of the creation is love."

"Strong and content I travel the open road,
Of physiology from top to toe I sing.
I think all heroic deeds were conceived in the open air.
Now I think I see the making of the best of persons:
It is to grow in the open air, and to eat and to sleep
    with the earth.

"Afoot and light-hearted I take to the open road,
Healthy, free, the world before me,
The long brown path before me, leading wherever I
    choose.
Henceforth I ask not good-fortune—I myself am
    good-fortune;
Henceforth I whimper no more, postpone no more,
    need nothing;
Strong and content I travel the open road.
    .   .   .   .

"A song of the good green grass,
A song no more of the city streets;
A song of farms—a song of the toil of fields,
A song with the smell of sun-dried hay, where the
    nimble pitchers handle the pitchfork;
A song tasting of new wheat, and of fresh-husked
    maize."

Journeying along the byways of mortal life, people generally find what they seek for. If they seek inviting groves and roses along the way, they find them,
and if they hunt for thorns, they find them. Whitman sought and sung of the good. While "on the
road" he looked up to suns, to stars, and not downward
into pits and mudholes of filth.

"None has understood you, but I understand you,
None has done justice to you; you have not done
    justice to yourself,
None but has found you imperfect, I only find no im-
    perfection in you."

Down to the inmost core, the divine Ego, the God incarnate under all the cells, monads and bodily rubbish, there is nothing but purity and perfection. Such is my deep conviction. The Westminster Confession phrase, "elect infants," with its corollary, "total depravity," was a piece of ecclesiastical wretchedness worthy of only a Scandinavian demon.

"Weep not, child,
  With these kisses let me remove your tears.
  The ravening clouds shall not long possess the sky,
      they devour the stars only in apparition,
  Jupiter shall emerge, be patient, watch again another
      night, the Pleiades shall emerge,
  They are immortal, all those stars, both silvery and
      golden shall shine out again,
  The great stars and the little ones shall shine out
      again, they endure
  The vast immortal suns and the long-enduring pensive
      moons shall again shine.
  None are lost. Souls that sink, re-born shall rise
      again."

How tender these words to his mother!

"Behold a woman!
  She looks out from her quaker cap, her face is clearer
      and more beautiful than the sky.
  She sits in an armchair under the shaded porch of the
      farmhouse,
  The sun just shines on her old white head.
  Her ample gown is of cream-hued linen,
  Her grandsons raised the flax, and her grand-daughters spun it with the distaff and the wheel,
  The melodious character of the earth,
  The finish beyond which philosophy cannot go and
      does not wish to go,
  The justified mother of men."

But why do I quote so freely from Walt Whitman?

Because I personally knew him—because I admired his personality—because I appreciated in a measure, at least, the spiritual wealth of his soul. It is by no means claimed that his verse is polished and rounded like Virgil's, or Milton's, Tennyson's or Longfellow's. He was not a copyist. Putting fashion under his feet, he bowed to no shrine of either pattern or patent. He was original. He was rugged as nature itself. His landscapes knew the touch of no foreign artists. His aim was not to display pictures but to create an atmosphere of inspiration, equality and brotherhood.

Men's estimates of him necessarily differ. Each naturally speaks or writes from his own mental and moral standpoint. Mr. Ernest Marklew, editing a Spiritualist journal in Preston, England, called *"The Medium,"* pronounces Walt Whitman *"an inconsequential piece of piebald humbug!"* Such an outburst of unwisdom is its own comment. In contrast, the Rev. Dr. Savage, one of the most learned and brilliant Unitarian orators in the Unitarian church of New York, says in his sermon, "A Plea For a Restful Life:" "And so, Walt Whitman, a man so misunderstood by the illiterate of his time, is going to take rank as one of the greatest creative forces in American literature. He would spend a large part of his time in what some would call idleness. Yet meanwhile, he was observing, gathering thoughts into his soul that when expressed would make the world richer, and vastly better." The critic of "the twelve great poets," speaks of Whitman as one of them—"a star in the firmament of poesy, whose fame grows with advancing years."

Years had passed since first meeting him, but occasionally I had read some of his added "leaves"—literally prose-poems, which flowed from his soul as rippling waters from hill-side fountains. The fervor of his hand-clasp had not faded from my memory. Friendships based upon principle are as abiding as the constellations of the heavens.

Later, supplying the Unitarian pulpit a few times in Camden, N. J., during the absence of their pastor, and learning that Whitman, an invalid, was in the city stopping with a friend, I made haste to call upon him. Entering his library-room where he was reclining in a large arm-chair, he extended the pale hand. His salutation was—"We have met before; souls do not forget." Whether in those words he referred to our meeting in Washington, or to a meeting in some pre-existent state of consciousness I do not know, but do know that he believed in the continuity of life—life past, present and future as the one life in the circle of being.

Recognizing his infirmity, gladly did I defer to his lead in the conversation. Though ill, his voice was strong, his eye clear, his intellect commanding and his personality morally imperial. His room was a veritable swamp of pamphlets, manuscripts and books. Half apologizing, he remarked, "This is my workshop, the tools lying around loosely; chaos, you know, precedes cosmos, and scattering timbers, work on the building."

His hair was nearly as white as the winter snows of our extreme northlands, reminding me that I had hear him spoken of as "the good, gray poet."

Referring to the reading of his "Leaves" with such emotion and grace by Mrs. Farnham, he remarked— "Woman—a woman's voice. She understood me. We are all coming to know each other better. Individual-

ity, races, nations, are gradually melting into one great
brotherhood.''

Following these calm inspirational words he pointed
me to this leaf in his book of leaves, referring, no
doubt to the Nazarene, so often called by the Evange-
lists the "son of man"—"the man of sorrows:"

"My spirit to yours, brother,
  Do not mind because many sounding your name do
    not understand you,
  I do not sound your name, but I understand you,
  I specify you with joy, O my comrade, to salute you,
    and to salute those who are with you, before and
    since, and those to come also,
  That we all labor together transmitting the same
    charge and succession,
  We few equals indifferent of lands, indifferent of
    times,
  We, enclosers of all continents, all castles, allowers
    of all theologies,
  Compassionaters, perceivers, rapport of men,
  We walk silent among disputes and assertions, but
    reject not the disputers nor anything that is
    asserted,
  We hear the brawling and din, we are reached at by
    divisions, jealouses, recriminations on every
    side,
  They close peremptorily upon us to surround us, my
    comrade,
  Yes we walk unheld, free, the whole earth over, jour-
    neying up and down till we make our ineffable
    mark upon time and the divers eras.
  Till we saturate time and eras, that the men and
    women of races, ages to come, may prove breth-
    ren and lovers as we are.''

Whitman was literally a giant of soul impulse.
There was not a shadow of sham about him. He was

innocent of fashion and affectation. "I am," he said, "but an idea—a spirit—a new language for Civilization. What am I but you, and what are you again but this same I, the two halves of a circle in an infinite circle."

He wrote of life as he saw it "on the road." Fame was to him a bubble to be shunned. Thousands admired both his personality and his verse. Some mocked. He heard the taunt—the jeer—the heartless scoff; but not heeding, he continued "on the road." Now better appreciated, he is receiving unstinted praise from this and foreign lands. Wrapt in admiration of him, I fancy that I can almost hear him from his sublime abode now repeating his inspired words:

"All seems beautiful to me,
I can repeat over to men and women, You have done
    such good to me I would do the same to you,
I will recruit for myself and you as I go,
I will scatter myself among men and women as I go,
I will toss a new gladness and roughness among them,
Whoever denies me it shall not trouble me,
Whoever accepts me, he or she shall be blessed, and
    shall bless me."

Whitman was eminently social. Horace Traubel, in his recent work, gives us most interesting descriptions of his letters and talks with the great men of his time. John Hay, our late world-famed Secretary of State, was very fond of him, as their correspondence proves. Longfellow called upon Whitman with Childs. Afterwards, our "good, gray poet" said, "Longfellow's manners were stately, conventional—all right but all careful."

"Was his conversation striking? Was he at all like Emerson?"

2

"Not at all. Emerson was as different as day from night. He had the best manners of any man I ever met; by this I mean manners in the right sense: manners, words, thoughts, always right, yet never at any time suggesting preparation or design. Emerson always seemed to know what he wanted. If I was asked to put him into two words I should give 'sincerity' first and then 'definiteness:' yes, sincerity and definiteness. Emerson never lost these qualities. In his last days, when it was said his 'mind had failed,' he remained of this aspect: in fact, it seemed to me to be empha-sized. Emerson only lost the outward, the superficial —the rest of him remained untouched. I thought Al-cott had really lost something. He came to see me in Brooklyn once, just before Emerson. While Emerson was with me I asked him about this breakdown of mem-ory or what-not in Alcott, but Emerson would not have it my way. He was gentle, but firm.

"The world does not know what our relations, Emerson's and mine, were. They think of our friend-ship always as a literary friendship: it was a bit that, but it was mostly something else—it was certainly more than that—for I loved Emerson for his personality and I always felt that he loved me for something I brought him from the rush of the big cities and the mass of men. We used to walk together, dine together—argue, even, in a sort of a way, though neither one of us was much of an arguer. We were not much for repartee, or sallies, or what people ordinarily call humor, but we got along together beautifully—the atmosphere was always sweet, I don't mind saying it, both on Emerson's side and mine: we had no friction—there was no kind of fight in us for each other—we were like two Quakers together. Dear Emerson! I doubt if the literary classes which have taken to coddling him, have any right to their god. He belonged to us—yes, to us—rather than to them." Then after a pause: "I suppose to all as well as to us—perhaps to no clique whatever—aye, to the wide—wide world."

Never shall the writer forget the afternoon that he spent with Emerson in his library. It was to me literally a "red-letter" day. It was he that, turning to volume after volume, rare and ancient, gave me the first impulse to the study of oriental literature.

Whitman was a child of nature. He loved alike the loneliness of the forest, the surging throngs along Broadway—the shoutings of children by the roadside and the singing of crickets in the gray of evening time. He was equally at home studying a sunset, riding upon the top of an omnibus, among the convicts of a prison, or sitting in a Quaker church. He was an all-around man, shunning the shallows of fashion and daring the roughness of life. His peerless presence was like a dynamo—radiating vigor and health, peace and good will.

The Rev. J. Page Hopps, the cultured and popular Unitarian preacher of London, author, scholar, and manly out-spoken Spiritualist, in speaking of the inspirations of Walt Whitman in *London Light* of April 28th, says:

"Surely it was the Holy Ghost, the Comforter, who inspired Walt Whitman to write these lovely lines in his 'Carol' for death:

Come, lovely and soothing death,
Undulate round the world, serenely arriving, arriving,
In the day, in the night, to all, to each,
Sooner or later, delicate death.

Dark Mother, always gliding near, with soft feet,
Have none chanted for thee a chant of fullest welcome?
Then I chant it for thee—I glorify thee above all;
I bring thee a song that, when thou must indeed come,
    come unfalteringly.

Over the tree-tops I float thee a song!
Over the rising and sinking waves—over the myriad
    fields and the prairies wide;
Over the dense-packed cities all, and the teeming
    wharves and ways,
I float this carol with joy, with joy to Thee, O Death!

Death is only an incident—a wave upon the measureless ocean of time—a burnished link in the chain of of eternal being. It is more—it is the new birth. Step lightly; spirit friends have come to attend this higher birth. See—they have brought garments bright and glistening. The stillness is holy and heavenly. The atmosphere is fragrant with the odors of the heavens. The dying, catching a glimpse of the loved in waiting—smile—there's now a tremor, the life-thread is severed and the light of eternity dawns upon the new-born, the twice-born son of the Eternal.

"Light of the universe
When shall I return me to Thee?
When shall I go back into the ancient places,
The paradise bowers of primeval love
My spirit longs for the antecedent home."

                        J. M. Peebles, M. D.

PREFACE.

The question of the nature and origin of the human spirit has occupied the thoughts more or less of the world's best thinkers through all the old agone ages.

Did the spirit begin to exist with the mortal body as a conscious individuality? Is it evolved from the physical body? Did it ascend up from protoplasmic slime through all the lower orders of creation? Did it begin to exist in time and space; or is it an incarnation —a spiritual implantation—a spark from the great Deific fire—a potentialized portion of God? These questions are considered and discussed in this book, which we send forth trustingly hoping that it may incite to still deeper thought, enlarge the sphere of human wisdom, and so enlighten and richly bless the world.

Pre-existence is, with myself, a settled conviction. But the pre-existence of the spirit is not the synonym of reincarnation. This latter, though somewhat germane, points to another field of investigation, the arguments in favor of which when lifted up out of the mire of oriental speculations, are growing in favor with me. Nevertheless, my final word has not been spoken upon this momentous subject.

Aye—will—*can* this word final ever be spoken. I almost tremble at the word finality. Is there any finality except in God—the Immutable—the Infinite?

Human life may be considered a pilgrimage, and this world a temporary tavern by the way, wherein we tarry for a time for experiences and discipline. Often the feet are pierced with thorns, the limbs are weary, the heart heavy, and the spirit lonely with the journeys, trials and tragedies, reminding us of John the Baptist's trance-vision of Jesus of Nazareth as pictured by the poet:

"He hath gone to the vineyard alone; is there
          no one to help?"
A voice—"There is none; He must gather alone."
    "He treadeth the winepress alone; is there
          none to help?"
A voice—"There is none; He must tread it alone."
    "He hath gone against the dragon alone; is
          there no one to help?"
A voice—"There is none; He must conquer alone."
    "Grief's archers sore press Him alone; is
          there no one to help?"
A voice—"There is none; He must suffer alone."
    "Death's sorrows o'erwhelm him alone; is
          there no one to help?"
A voice—"There is none; He is victor alone."
    "Hell's legions assail him alone; is there
          no one to help?"
A voice—"There is none; He shall triumph alone."

Exalted minds dwell in the element of the spiritual. The spiritual is the real. Poets are the soul's prophets. Jesus was a poet, prophet and rabbi. They are unlike metaphysicians; they give us the product of their spiritual life, and intuitive insight and appeal to the consciousness and deep sympathies of humanity for the verification. Poets are divinely appointed interpreters, employing the shadows of the outer-world to re-

veal the substance of the world within. All along
down the pages of thought and culture, from the Vedic
hymns of the Hindus, their glory gleams in the brightness of divine truth, and their lines, ever tender, glow
with the fadeless radiance of immortal love. Here is a
sample:

"Before the solar systems were conceived,
When nothing was but the unnamable,
My spirit lived, an atom of the Cause,
Through countless ages and in many forms
It had existed ere it entered in
This human frame to serve its little day
Upon the earth. The deathless Me of me,
The spark from that great all-creative fire,
Is part of that eternal source called God,
And mightier than the Universe."

       —Ella Wheeler Wilcox.

THE SPIRIT'S PATHWAY TRACED.

DO HUMAN SPIRITS PRE-EXIST?

AND

DO THEY AGAIN REINCARNATE?

BY

J. M. PEEBLES, M. D.

CHAPTER I.

THE PRE-EXISTENCE OF THE SPIRIT.

There are few scholars, and probably no profound philosophers who do not distinguish and note the difference between the words "soul" and "spirit." Paul did when he wrote—"I pray God to preserve you body, soul and spirit." And the Roman Marcus Aurelius did when urging that life was a unit—that the sensations were subjective, and that the "soul (soul-body) was a refined, corporeal organism."

The learned Alford in his Greek Testament states that *Pneuma* is the highest and persistent part of man, while the *Psuche,* the lower or animal soul, contains the desires and passions which we have in common with the brutes.

Prof. Schubert, a follower of Schelling, states that "the soul is the inferior part of every intellectual nature, the interior organism, while the spirit is that part of our nature which tends to the purely rational, the spiritual and the divine."

In common parlance it is said "the sun rises," and that "the soul is immortal," yet the astronomer knows that the sun does not rise, and so the philosopher and the cultured theologian know that the soul is not immortal, for while it is attenuated it is also particled, changeable and may die. Hence, the old biblical passage, "The soul that sinneth it shall die." The soul, or soul-body, is the vehicle, the tabernacle in which the spirit—the immortal spirit tents and manifests during its mortal pilgrimage. It is the conscious spirit that is immortal and pre-existent. "But," rejoins someone, *"Non mi ricordo."* (I do not remember.) Granted, but that does not disprove an eternal past existence. You do not remember your past foetal life, nor your nine months placenta life; nor do you remember your baby life nor your early childhood life. But this counts for nothing against your existence during all these periods. You nevertheless have access to an ample amount of evidence that your existence traversed all these stages—evidence that your personality was prior to your conscious memory of it.

Because this inmost spirit cannot project itself through its clumsy, clayish environment into the external with sufficient vividness to remember the past and express it in human language, is no evidence that the individualized spirit did not exist. Non-existence is unthinkable. And thinking is as natural as breathing. Only circles are endless. All beginnings in time and space necessarily have their endings. A creature which has had its full beginning in time is incapable of perpetuating itself or of being perpetuated through eternity. A line projected from a point in space has a further geometrical limit which no logic can carry to infinitude. Whether or not "God geometrizes," that cannot be morally and psychologically false which is mathematically true. Though on different planes of thought, morals and mathematics harmonize. The universe is not a dual-verse of infinite inharmonies, but a unit of harmonies, not fathomed nor fully understood.

I may here remark that two fundamental assumptions lie at the threshold of man's introduction into this world. The first is, that his subjective existence ante-dates his objective appearance. That as an ego he is co-existent with the universe, and participates in that universal and eternal life which is perpetually manifest in the cosmos.

The second assumption, is that man as to his essential form or inmost individuality is derivative; that his earliest introduction into the world and the universe is when he is born of a physical mother; that his conscious individuality is dependent upon and dates its beginning with the visible appearance of the physical organism. According to this assumption the material atoms and forces which have transiently converged in the human organism, with no promise or purpose of anything more than a limited persistence, were once conglomerated with the great cosmic mass as a portion of its unorganized, undifferentiated substance. And this hypothesis of derivatived man further assumes that the purpose, if there were any, of this single existence is to specialize a portion of the organizable pabulum of the general cosmos into human shape, that it may in some way manifest the attributes of self-consciousness. This materialistic hypothesis still further assumes that the inmost individuality co-existent with this body-organism, commenced its existence with it, and must have its share in its vicissitudes and logically its final destruction. Is it surprising that such a materialistic philosophy should yield its abundant crop of uneasy atheists?

With the wisest of the Greek philosophers, diversity, individuality, was as fundamental as unity; but with our modern scientists, the Ego, the conscious individuality is purely derivative. The Darwinian school of writers assume that our world and solar system, together with the kingdoms of life, nay, even the genius of Homer, Raphael and Shakespeare were "once latent in a fiery cloud." All specific forms, say they, came by development, they arose by insensible modifications wrought in an originally homogenous substance. That also was the philosophy of certain ancient Hindus. That was the philosophy of Spinoza. That, too, is in a degree the philosophy of Herbert Spencer and of Darwin's disciples. Darwin's qualification to the effect that God originally, and, I may add, miraculously, created a "few germs," as a basis from which to evolve future distinctions and organic formations, does not redeem his theory from that pantheistic conception which is its very root and essence. It is, in fact, the pantheism of rankest materialism.

Spinoza and the pantheistic philosophers of India taught this in harmony with the logical implications of their philosophy. They were materialists; inasmuch as types, or essential forms, with them, were not co-existent with substance, but effects, or derivative results, consequent upon the differentiation and integration of substance; so these beginnings necessitated endings. Forms were ephemeral. They were particled; hence, their destiny was to suffer resolution into the primitive substance.

Future immortality logically implies a pre-exist-

ent, or past, immortality. And any attempt to reconcile man's future immortality with Darwinism, or with
any form of materialism, is much like Hugh Miller's
effort to reconcile geology and Genesis. It seems clear
to the reasoner that if a protoplastic formation without intelligent force originated, evolved and built up
essential man, involving the personal identity, the con-
cious Ego, it may, and necessarily must, by the law of
involution, and atomic changes return again to protoplasm.

It was precisely upon this point that Agassiz took
issue with Darwin. The former held with Plato that
ideas and ultimate forms were co-existent with substance. He taught that they had a spiritual basis, ante-
dating their material embodiments. It is not sufficient
to say that man existed in essence before he became a
personal identity. If that identity was produced, if it
be a result, an effect, consequent upon molecular action,
or material change, then no "key-stone" in the arch-
way of organization will insure that identity from final
resolution into that "fiery cloud," in which Tyndal informs us the genius of Raphael and Shakespeare were
once latent.

A marked distinction must be made between Darwinism and evolution. The higher evolution in connection with involution harmonizes with the spirit's
upward career. The arc implies the balance of forces.

Individuals favoring the Darwinian school of materialism and believing in derivative individuality, ask
for facts in proof of pre-existence, by which they
doubtless mean facts addressed to the perceptive intellect, but I submit that facts of the sensuous order are
quite incompetent to prove or disprove truths which
address themselves to intuition and the highest reason.

To me the facts of consciousness and intuition are far
more authoritative and imperial than those appealing
to the fallible senses.

Scholars, thinkers and metaphysicians of all schools
recognize three orders of evidence which may be com-
petent to influence the judgment.

1.   Evidence addressed to the senses—sense perceptions.

2.   Evidence addressed to the rational and conscious understanding.

3.   Evidence addressed to the moral reason in the
form of axioms and intuitions.

The demand for facts of external observation in
proof of those higher truths of recondite relations and
of that consciousness which can only be apprehended
by the higher reason, will not be gratified; at least in
the present condition of our worldly humanity. The
problem of pre-existence is included in the provinces of
consciousness, mental science, metaphysics and religion, rather than in that of the physical sciences. Science may afford important aid by revealing the laws of
movement; but its sphere being limited to the order
and sequence of physical phenomena, it can never reveal the vital nature of things in themselves. I have
no expectation that the problem of man's first estate
will ever have any clear light thrown upon it by re-
course to such data as material science will be able to
furnish, for it involves an ultimate ground that lies beyond the pale of the microscope and experimental research. And then what is denominated science today
is pronounced non-science in the next decade.

A strong presumptive evidence in favor of the truth
of a proposition is to be found in the extent of its dif-
fusion and in the degree of its persistence. This is an

axiomatic truth with Herbert Spencer. Now the belief in the spirit's pre-existence—the belief in God and the immortality of man have survived the rise and fall of empires, thrones and powerful races. Nor has modern enlightenment succeeded in driving them into the dreamy haunts of superstition and materialism, but it has welcomed, extended and fortified these beliefs. They may be accepted, therefore, as foreshadowing, or rather, as the synonyms of ultimate verities.

CHAPTER II.

OUR CONCEPTION OF THE HUMAN SPIRIT.

Sankaramarya, an illustrious oriental poet, in attempting to define universal spirit—pure essential spirit, wrote thus:

"I am neither body nor changes of the body;
Nor am I senses or object of the senses.

"I am neither temple nor worship;
Nor pilgrimage nor books. I am life.

"I have neither death nor fear of death;
Nor was I ever born, nor had I parents.

"I am not misery, nor ever had I misery;
I am not enemy, nor had I enemies.

"I am without limit, beyond space, beyond time;
I am in everything; I am the basis of the universe;
everywhere I am Existence Absolute; Knowledge
Absolute; Will Absolute; Bliss Absolute;
I enternally was—am—and eternally shall be."

Poets in their more inspired moments of exaltation often sing of pre-existence:

"I have dreamed
Of sinless men and maids, mated in heaven
Ere yet their souls had sought for beauteous forms
To give them human sense and residence."
—*Holland.*

I believe the spirit, the Ego, to be an eternal entity, or unit from all eternity. The spirit is immortal and has its state of being within God. The spirit is absolute. Nothing can be taken from it or added to it. Its manifestations in time proceed from sources that are within. The spirit in its inmost quality is like unto God. It is a ray which proceeds from God as a mighty central sun. Its being is in God, and yet it is not God. The chandelier lights the furniture in the parlor, but neither the furniture nor the vibrations are the light-giving chandelier. The essential nature of God cannot be communicated through the medium of poor human speech, for it is only known within the spirit. Knowledge proceeds from the known to the unknown. The life, the consciousness of the universe is God; the consciousness of man is the spirit.

The spirit is the only pre-existing entity except God, having its being in eternity and its existence in time. Existing in time the spirit is subject to limitations, but God is the Absolute Being transcending all limitations. The spirit geometrically expressed, is a complete circle, having neither beginning nor ending. God is the sphere in which the circle is related to infinity. But while the spirit abides in the Infinite it is never lost therein. Annihilation is both unthinkable and impossible. There are probably no new spirits added to the universe; none taken therefrom. The spirit in its primal nature does not exist in time or space, but in eternity. Only its movements or manifestations fall within the province of time and space. It unfolds in manifestation, but *not* in essential quality.

It will hence be seen that the spirit in its first estate

is a purely, and germinally a subjective being in the
human form. In this primal state it embodies all the
attributes and spiritual qualities which we can conceive of as embraced in the cosmos. It is Plato's "One
and Many"—a unity in which is embraced multitudes.
All numbers, forms, forces and series inhere in this
microcosmic entity. Love, wisdom and will constitute
the spiritual substance and form of its existence. Love
is its inmost substance and the subjective ground of its
being. Wisdom is its form of existence and quality of
limitation, while self-determined will is the conscious
force that distinguishes it from all other human entities. Considered in one aspect the infinite multitude
of spirits in the universe form one complex and unitary
body, each sharing the same divine qualities with his
fellow, which is the ground of their sociality. It is
also the ground of universal brotherhood. But viewed
in another aspect, spirits present an infinite diversity,
no two being precisely alike, nor predestined to per-
form identical offices. Thus all spirits cohere in social
solidarity by virtue of the principle of love which inheres alike in each. And then again, each spirit is a
Form *per se,* distinguished from all others by virtue
of its principle of Wisdom or quality of limitation.
Accordingly, each spirit is endowed with a specialty
of genius which qualifies it for a particular function
and form of service, as a unit in the affiliated series of
the universal life. But before the spirit can become
equipped to consciously serve in its pre-destined place
in the universe, it must perfect for itself a soul-form
or etheric body, through which it can fully express its
subjective wealth of faculty. This soul-form will be
the ultimate, the final summing up of the spirit's pilgrimages in and through matter.

"A keel grated on the sand,
  Then a step was on the shore—
Life awoke and heard it.
A hand was laid upon her,
And a great shudder passed through her.
She looked up, and saw over her
The strange, wide eyes of Love,
And life knew for whom
She had been waiting,
And Love drew Life up to him,
And of that meeting was born
A thing rare and beautiful—
Joy, First Joy was it called."
                    Olive Schreinrer.

Prof. Larkin in his scholarly book "Radiant Energy," informs us that "matter and energy are all that have been found during three centuries of incessant research in all that portion of the Universe visible in a forty-inch telescope, and armed with the most powerful spectroscope made."

With all due deference to astronomical science, the forty-inch telescope and the spectroscope have found neither matter, nor energy. They have only found manifestations—found visible forms called matter, and an invisible force called energy, something such as is manifest in a land-slide, or a boulder bounding, rushing down a mountain-side. Astronomical and mathematical instruments know nothing of consciousness, or intuition, or the higher reason, neither can they reveal what does not inhere in them.

The position of this professor reminds me of a Chicago surgeon, a materialist, who gravely informed me that he had dissected scores of cadavers, cutting their brains all to atoms, yet finding there no immortal spirit. "Quite likely," was my reply, adding inquiringly, "did you find any thoughts there that flamed for expression—any ideas there that aspired to mental and moral eminence?" There was silence then. The unseen, rather than the seen, is the abiding reality. Phenomena are ephemeral appearances, but the unseen, the noumenal are the real and the substantial.

To convey an idea of the potency and durability of unseen essences, consider the tuberose, or what is more potent, the Persian moss-rose, which will flood a drawing-room with a most delightful fragrance for weeks.

A grain of musk placed in and diffused through a room will remain for an indefinite time, as the nasal passages testify.

Particles of odorous substance in the act of smelling, produce molecular changes, which transferred through nerve fibres to the nerve centers of sensation, report to consciousness. It is clear to the writer that being conscious of our consciousness we know more of consciousness than we do of the clay under our feet, more of mind than we do of matter, and more of the invisible spiritual man than we do of the physical that measurably besets and binds us.

Although not absolute proof, yet the most illustrious prophets, poets, sages and philosophers of the past were ardent believers in the spirit's pre-existence. On the other hand, materialists, and a few noted thinkers not only deny, but with a sarcasm that stings they intellectually trample the theory under their feet. Among them is that clear-headed thinker and writer— a writer that however we may differ in opinion, I am proud to consider and honor as a friend—W. Emmette Coleman. What this author and student of analytical philosophy has not said and cannot say, cannot, in my opinion, be said against pre-existence.

In reviewing or noticing the book entitled "Demonism of The Ages and Spirit Obsessions," a number of distinguished persons are named who repudiate the doctrine of pre-existence; and an equal, aye, a much larger number, beginning with Prof. Alexander Wilder, and Prof. E. Whipple, and Prof. Kiddle, can be named who accept it.

Prof. Wm. Knight, of St. Andrews, Edinburg University, in a very able essay, published in the *Fortnightly Review,* thus speaks of the doctrine of pre-existence: "Its root," says he, "is the indestructibility of the vital principle. Let a belief in pre-existence be joined to that of posthumous existence, and the dogma is complete. It is thus at one and the same time a theory of the soul's origin and of its destination, and its unparalleled hold upon the human race may be explained in part by the fact of its combining both in a single doctrine. . . . It is probably the most widespread and permanently influential of all speculative theories as to the origin and destination of the soul. . . . It has lain at the heart of all Indian speculation on the subject, time out of mind. It is one of the cardinal doctrines of the Vedas, one of the roots of Buddhist belief. The ancient Egyptians held it. In Persia it colored the whole stream of Zoroastrian thought. The Magi taught it. The Jews brought it with them from their captivity in Babylon. Many of the Essenes and Pharisees held it. . . . The Apocrypha sanctions it, and it is to be found scattered throughout the Talmud. In Greece Pythagoras proclaimed it; Empedocles taught it, Plato worked it elaborately out, not as a mythical doctrine embodying a moral truth, but as a philosophical theory or conviction. It passed over into the Neo-Platonic school at Alexandria. Philo held it.

Plotinus and Porphyry in the third century, Jamblichus in the fourth, Hierocles and Proclus in the fifth, all advocated it in various ways. Many of the fathers of the Manicheans received it, with much else, from their Zoroastrian predecessors. It was held by Nemesius, who emphatically declares that all the Greeks who believe in immortality believe also in pre-existence. There are hints of it in Boethius. It was defended with much learning and acuteness by several of the Cambridge Platonists, especially by Henry More. Glanville devotes a curious treatise to it, the *Lux Orientalis;* English clergy and Irish bishops were found ready to espouse it. Poets, from Henry Vaughn to Wordsworth praise it. It won the passing suffrage of Hume, as more rational than the rival theories of Creation and Tradition. It was held by Swedenborg, and it has points of contact with the anthropology of Kant and Schelling. It found an earnest advocate in Lessing. Herder also maintained it, while it fascinated the minds of Fourier and Leroux. Soame Jenyus, the Chevalier Ramsay and the erudite Edward Cox have written in its defense.''

This erudite writer, Mr. Coleman, in criticising my belief in pre-existence, submits the following:

''If the soul has been eternally existent, what has it been doing all through the ages? Progress being the order of nature, we should think that by this time it would have attained to the most exalted intellectual, moral, and spiritual grandeur, beyond the highest conceptions of our undeveloped minds; yet we find these godlike spirits, when they enter this world, in many cases just a degree above the brute,—mere biped brutes, coarse, ignorant savages and barbarians.

Dr. Peebles has told told us that all the pre-existent

souls from all eternity revel in "ecstatic bliss' proir to their incarnation in material bodies. By what strange metamorphosis does a God of the upper heavens become transformed into an Australian, a Fiji Islander, or a Bosjesman (or Bushman)? If these souls have been in an 'ecstatic' state for myriads of ages, whence the utility of their becoming inhabitants of animal bodies on earth, filled with base passions and groveling instincts, and compelled to take with them, at death, to the spirit world, their depraved natures, there having, by persistent effort, to outgrow their debasing habits of thought and mind consequent upon their life on earth? How is it that these exalted spirits become the obsessing demons that Dr. Peebles so strenuously insists upon as causing so much harm on earth? Do these heavenly entities voluntarily abandon their ecstatic paradisian home, and willingly descend to earth to become Hottentots, Esquimaux, Aleutian Islanders and Digger Indians: and what justice is there in some of these spirits being incarnated as brutes and savages, while others become a Shakespeare, a Spencer, a Washington, or a Peebles?"

The above from the trenchant pen of the scholarly Coleman is little more than a bundle of assertions, accompanied by a series of questions, which may be successfully answered by another series equally as potent. For instance, where was this writer Coleman and "what was he doing" when this earth was a liquid, seething mass of fiery fluid? or where was he when it was being transformed into rocks, into soils, mosses, rushes and ferns? Was he wrapped in the soil as are worms and insects? Did he grow up out of the earth as did mushrooms and insects? Certainly not.

Briefly then, did he as a conscious spirit at this time exist—*pre-exist?* If not, then we have the miracle— the astounding 20th century miracle, of existence from non-existence—somebody from nobody—something from nothing: Coleman from the gaping womb of non-entity. Let no one who accepts this theory stagger hereafter at the old churchianic dogma that the world was made in six twenty-four-hour days out of nothing. The old Latin maxim of Lucretius' time, *ex-nihilo nihil fit,* from nothing nothing comes—stands like a rock amid all the materialistic subtleties of the centuries.

What was the pre-existent spirit doing "all through the ages," ask these inquisitors.

Candidly, I do not know. Neither do I know what I was doing a year after my birth, nearly 85 years ago; nor do I know what ever became of my baby hair. I do not know what I was doing when soundly asleep last night, yet I am very certain that I existed.

To be more explicit, the chandelier, though illuminating everything in the room, does not vibrate, does not shine out through the compact brick wall. Such projection is impossible. What in all time past, I, as a spirit, was thinking—or what, as a germinal psychic, environed in the barriers of etheric sensuous substance, or in the various grades and limitations of matter—I was doing, I do not now vividly remember. These grosser mortal barriers do and ever did limit the area —the expression of the spirit's consciousness. In line with this thought, Prof. Tyndall in his Belfast address said: "You cannot satisfy the human understanding in its demand for logical continuity between molecular processes and the phenomena of consciousness. This is a rock on which materialism must inevitably split whenever it pretends to be a complete philosophy of life." And Dubois-Raymond said that "consciousness, not originating in matter, cannot, owing to the non-sensibility of matter, perfectly express itself through it, or through physical forms related to it."

"By what strange metamorphosis," asks Mr. Coleman, "does a god of the upper heavens become transformed into an Australian, Bosjesman or Bushman?"
Possibly by the reverse method that the evolution-god
of the hells transformed amoeba, worms, kanga-
roos and monkeys into degraded Anglo-Saxon men.
Touching this theory I am decidedly skeptical. I trace
my spirit ancestry to God, called by the prophet "the
father of all spirits," rather than to apes and baboons,
who through unexplained transformations become
men. There is something grand beyond grandeur
itself in a conscious spirit's descent into matter for,
as the Neo-Platonists taught, experiences on another
plane of consciousness—experiences that may be priceless in teaching the relation of causes to their effects.
What a spirit thinks as a spirit unfleshed is not remembered only in the rarest cases by a spirit enveloped and
hemmed in by fleshly prison walls.

The following paragraph by friend Coleman requires a word of notice:

"Many Spiritualists have taught that a great deal
of the insanity of the world is caused by obsessing,
evil spirits, and that these insane persons can be cured
by the exorcism of the evil spirits infesting the poor
unfortunates. What a repulsive idea, and, to my mind,
how repugnant to common sense!"

There is no timidity in these words. Emphatically,
"many Spiritualists" (such as that illustrious jurist,
Judge Edmonds, Prof. Kiddle, Prof. Brittan, Prof. E.
Whipple and others distinguished for investigation
and patient research) have taught that much of the
insanity of the country is caused by the obsession of
unwise, evil-disposed spirits. But: "What a repulsive idea!" exclaims Mr. Coleman. Yes—it is as

repulsive as is Spiritualism itself to many sectarian ecclesiastics. Pronouncing well-established obsessional facts "repulsive" (a child's argument), does not an- nihilate the facts. The candid inquiry of the scientist and the philosopher is this: "Is it a fact? And if so pronounced by responsible persons, I will, throwing all prejudice aside, vigorously investigate the matter to the finish." Such a proposition is honorable.

While pre-existence is a fact accepted alike by the greatest number and by the greatest minds in the world, the descent of spirits into human forms (not "brutes," as Coleman uncharitably states and as some Buddhists believe) is a matter of choice.

Chance is not compatible with law. This universe implies a directive purpose rather than a catastrophe, and though exceedingly difficult for the plodding, selfish, commercial citizens to comprehend self-sacri- fice, self-humiliation to help others, self-forgetfulness to remember others, toiling for their good—these— this, is more than altruism; it is God manifest. De- scent from the heavens to aid others in ascent is the purest divinity that mortal or immortal can know or practise. Beautifully, inspirationally, wrote Tenny- son:

"Earth, those solid stars, this weight of body and
    limbs;
Are they not sign and symbol of thy division from
    Him?"
"Dark is the world to thee: thyself art the reason why;
For is He not all but that which has power to feel 'I
    am I'?"
"Speak to Him then for He hears, and spirit with
    spirit can meet.
Closer is He than breathing, and nearer than hands
    and feet."

CHAPTER III.

WHAT IS THE NATURE OF THE HUMAN SPIRIT THAT PRE-EXISTS?

"And in the spheral chime they listening heard
The soul's high destiny, which, being sunk
Into this fleeting life, through obscure paths
Must wander, fighting still a God-like fight—
Victor, through death!"
—*Schelling.*

This grand universe of which our planet forms a very small portion, is not an orphan, not a dice-throw, not a helter-skelter chance universe that somehow got itself into existence without plan or purpose. It is a universe of law and order—I repeat, of law and order, else no astronomer could foretell to the day and the hour for centuries ahead, the coming of an eclipse. The returning new moon, the revolution of the seasons, succession of day and night are all in evidence of law and order; and these manifestations indicate—demonstrate the realty of a Cause behind and within, adequate to their production. There is here no alternative. This universe, aglow with life and cosmic consciousness, was either the product of an intelligent purpose with executive power sufficient to actualize that pre-existing purpose, or it chanced itself—*chanced itself into being.* There is no middle ground here for metaphysical wriggling. Neither chance nor force is creative: the latter is only executive. Force relates to laws, but does not make them. Laws are not causes. Law is a mode of action, and to talk of law, or force, or motion, or protoplasm as the originating cause of consciousness, or reason, or immortality, is parrot talk and nothing more. Nothing could have come out of protoplasm that was not first potentially in it—and here again we have pre-existence.

Our academic days taught us that a body could not move where it was not. Is this true of the conscious spirit? Can it act where it is not? But spirits do act far away from the brain centers they normally inhabit, showing conclusively that they temporarily may leave their own cranial habitations. Somnambulism, dreams, trances and scientific hypnotism, such as is practiced at Nancy and Salpetviere in France, are in evidence that human consciousness can and does act apart from the body which it has built up to tabernacle in for a time.

The physical eye cannot see the human spirit, nor can the clairvoyant eye see it in its fulness nor describe it. Neither the microscope nor the hyper-microscope can get a glimpse of it. It does not pertain to the plane of the visible, nor belong to any series of geometrical dimensions. Often have I put questions like this to very high intelligences when they were entrancing sensitives: "Can you under any conditions see the real, conscious spirit of this influencing spirit friend?" and the reply has invariably been in the negative.

To be more explicit, frequently have I asked these invisible yet entrancing intelligences, who had previously stated that when they took control of the subject, the spirit normally connected with this sensitive, leaves the organism:

Is this a theory with you or is it a literal fact?

"It is a positive fact with our instrument, but I cannot go, or authoritatively speak beyond the domain of my personal observation and experience."

Where is the spirit that just at this time has temporarily vacated the organism for you to use?

"It is here, close by us, and in a kind of a sympathetic converse with other intelligences disrobed of mortality."

Can you see—can you describe this unclothed spirit?

"I cannot. The most that I can say is that it looks like a fiery diamond—a brilliant point of dazzling brightness shining through a very ethereal white film, and connected in some way (sympathetically and vibratorially) with the sensitive that I am now using. And I am sure that all life, all energy, all thought, centers in this spirit."

The forces that infill and influence crude matter are in a measure apprehensible, while the forces that influence more attenuated substance, known as living matter, are spiritual. And further, the forces and intelligent principles that developed the human body, exhibiting design in the structure, are independent of the matter, the monads and molecules composing it. Spirit molds matter. Spirits are master-builders. They form the bodies which they inhabit. If advanced enough in the comprehending and in the manipulation of the electrons, cells, nervo-circulation and the subjective soul-form, they can leave the body temporarily and return—leave it by request of some other spirit, for a purpose—leave it and dwell in another human body for a time, serving some good end thereby. Only an arch-bungler would build his house so hemming himself that he could not get out of it.

In confirmation of the above, that marvelous phenomenon known as the "Watseka Wonder" was and is an evidence, because a number of the friends, the Roffs and their relatives are still residents of Watseka, Ill.*

In this marked instance, the so-called dead Mary Roff entered into and lived for several months in the physical body of Lurancy Vennum. This household phenomenon was a temporary re-inhabiting, or the re-incarnation of a conscious rational spirit into another human body for the purpose of healing this other body, 'Rancy Vennum, and the allowing of Mary Roff the great pleasure of a renewed and more direct experience with her earthly friends yet vestured in mortality. During these months of the rehabitation of a mortal organization she talked much of heaven, of the conditions and occupations of those who had put off their bodies and had gone up one step higher, with better environments and opportunities for soul-unfolding.

Charles Dawbarn, termed the "Philosopher of the Pacific," insists that the minutest molecule is constructed of and aglow with "substance, energy and intelligence."

That eminent Eastern authority, Ashvalayama, taught that from the "Atma sprang the shadow, the material sheath, and that within this sheath-vehicle was the soul-form, or body, and that interior to this was pure intelligence, the spirit; and that above and over all was Absolute Being."

---

*N. B. It affords me much pleasure to state that I knew intimately this family of the Roff's, Mrs. Alter, a sister of Mary, and other relatives. I had been a guest in their hospitable home, and was for a time the physician of Mr. Roff, who had an enviable standing among his fellow-men as a man of intelligence and high moral integrity. The whole family was exemplary and cultured—known only to be esteemed and honored.

Parmenides, Grecian philosopher and adept, taught that the soul was "a compound of elements," while the "divine intelligence," the spirit, "was a unit and indestructible."

It is clear to my vision that this uncompounded, indivisible, eternal ego, the conscious "I am," eternally was and is a potentialized portion or principle of the infinite all-energizing spirit of the universe, and so, necessarily pre-existed before the material body.

The profound Synesius of Pentapolis wrote this in the Latin language:

"A fragment of the Divine Parent descended into
    matter;
A small portion indeed, but it is everywhere the One
    in all.
All diffused through all, it turns the vast circumfer-
    ence of heaven,
Preserving the universe: distributed in diverse forms,
    it is present.
A part of it is the course of the stars; a part is the
    angelic choir;
A part—with a heavy bond—found an earthly form."

Theodore Parker said in Music Hall, Boston, in 1875 (See Giles B. Stebbin's Bible of The Ages, p. 322), "We thank thee, O Father, for this atom of spirit, a particle from thine own flame of eternity which thou hast lodged in this clay."

And Longfellow in an inspired moment, sang:

"Our birth is but a sleep and a forgetting;
The soul that rises with us, our life's star,
    Has had elsewhere its setting,
    And cometh from afar,

Not in entire forgetfulness,
And not in utter nakedness,
But trailing clouds of glory, do we come
From God, who is our home.''

Some writers of materialistic tendencies have fren-
ziedly conveyed the wild idea that there was originally
nothing in this mighty and measureless universe except
matter and force, which two unknowables somehow got
into molecular affinity and struggled—and struggled
through an unconceivable past eternity to evolve a
savage man, the legitimate son of an orang-utang.
Until this matter—and—force amoeba appeared on its
way up through a serpentine brutehood to manhood, all
the vast spaces of infinity were naught but abysmal
emptiness—all, everything, was enzoned in the dreamless vacuum of nonentity, and oue of and up from which
without life, intelligence, consciousness or purpose,
there sprang into being through countless aeons of
time, savage, ape-like men.

Do I hear it said that in that past so remote that
figures fail to count, ''force was acting on matter?''
How does one know? What grounds have you for the
hypothesis? If at this time force acted on matter, what
caused the impulse, the blind force to act? If it was
not blind but intelligent, this would be coming squarely
into the Theistic ground of God, in whose immanence
all spirits incarnate or discarnate live and move and
have their being.

Considered from every point of view, the pre-existence of the spirit—the life-entity, the ''god-atom,'' as a
German writer terms it; the Ego, the Atma of the
Vedantist seems more than reasonable. To my conception it is axiomatic.

CHAPTER IV.

PRE-EXISTING INTERNAL OBSESSIONS.

"Weep for the god-like life we lost afar
That thou and I its scattered fragments are:
And still the unconquered yearning we retain,
And sigh to renew the long and vanished reign
And grow divine again."

—*Dryden.*

It is no more logical to affirm that the this implies the that, than that the external implies the thinking internal. Atoms were once thought to be fixed, indivisible entities and imperishable, but now they are being broken into thousands of pieces and they are loaded with energy. There is energy "enough in a pound of coal," says Prof. Dolbear of Tuft's College, "to raise itself a distance of 3,000 miles. A pound of hydrogen would raise itself 12,000 miles." Life forces are everywhere. There is no dead matter. The waste connected with the dying, the dissolving of organic bodies becomes vitalizing nourishment for lower forms. Nothing exists for itself alone. Interdependence and interaction are kept up between particles and worlds—a constant outgoing of vibratorous impulses and a returning reception of impressions.

Well do I remember the shouting plaudits of a wonder-stricken public when the discovery of "Bathy-

4   49

bius," a pronounced vitalizing substance extending, it was said, hundreds of thousands of miles over the bottom of the sea and from which as a protoplasmic base there sprang the lowest types of animal life. But the Challenger's brief song of "life from the sea—life from pre-existent death," dropped dead and was soon buried too deep for a resurrection.

Yes, the Darwinian's "Bathybius" died soon after being named. And now these long years after, not only Bathybius but the existence, the very existence of matter is being questioned, and so Berkeley, that illustrious metaphysical philosopher, is again to the front. What the majority term matter is considered by eminent biologists and psychologists to be substance—etheric substance, which infinitely attenuated stuff was and may be so manipulated and condensed in nature's crucible by law and the forces that relate to law, as to become clearly visible and weighty enough to become the subject of avoirdupois—matter!

Writers and thinkers of materialistic tendencies taught in the older centuries that originally there was nothing anywhere but unlimited void—sheer abysmal emptiness. Then it was contended at a much later period that there was nothing originally in the universe of space but matter and force, and force acting upon matter—but what started the acting we are not told—acting and struggling without intelligence, consciousness, purpose or wisely-directed Energy, evolved monerons, mammalia, monkeys, and ultimately aboriginal men. Again, something from nothing! Only a shriveled, unbalanced brain could have hatched out such a silly theory!

The existence and eternity of God as the infilling energy of all being is axiomatic, and the eternity of

substance—particled, etheric substance, is now generally admitted. To the intuitive well-balanced mind
this is self-evident. And these particles, essences, elements, entities, monads, atoms, motes, molecules, swarm
in incalculable numbers in the atmospheres and gases
that encircle us. These we inhale; and if each entity
inhaled is unitively held together by a central force—
and it is—are we not rapidly getting on towards internal obsessions?

In connection with this, carefully consider the matter of dust and floating motes. Let a ray of sunlight
stream through a keyhole into a dark room and an eye-
glance reveals to the sense-perceptions millions of
moving, whirling particles of dust.

Consider again the wind-driven dust of the streets
and the filthy lanes of cities, the smoke of factories, the
invisible floating malaria in wood-shaded valleys, in
low, foggy swamplands, the spores in drains, the bacteria, the unorganized elements in dark storehouses,
damp, ill-ventilated parlors, pool-rooms, dance-halls
and theatres; these—all these, are the abiding places
of micro-organisms, millions of which clustered together would not make a mass larger, we are told, than
a pin-head or a pea; and yet, they are entities breathed
and re-breathed, finding lodgment in the blood and
the tissues of the human body. And what is more,
these germs, these entities are not dead. Death, absolute death, can produce no effect. These entities do.
They obsess. They injure the health.

Here comes up the old objection—"no two things
can occupy the same space at the same time." Granted,
and what of it? Think a moment! The brain is an
electro-magnetic dynamo, converting electrical energy
into spiritual energy, conducted by the inhering con-

scious Ego—the one original indivisible spiritual
ruler. And this cranial area of the brain consists of a
congeries of convolutions; and further, as estimated,
it contains 12,000,000 of atomic cells, each cell being a
center of force. These cells are born, grow, die; releas-
ing the infinitesimal Egos temporarily imprisoned,
which may be attracted to the same brain or the same
body again, or may, by counter impelling attractions
enter the aura, the brain, the nerves, or blood corpuscles of another, and there remain until physically removed.

The average amount, of the all-too-often germ-
laden atmosphere taken into the lungs at each breath,
says Dr. Pruden, is thirty cubic inches. Basing our
estimates upon careful study and reliable reports, with
every twenty breaths one may take into his body all the
way from 11 to 376 living micro-organisms, real entities. Think of it—living micro-organisms taken into
the lungs, the blood, the body, the brain, the nerve
centers. And these, by French and German scientists,
are pronounced "alive—living." Do you not begin to
see the rationale of internal obsessions?

Stating nothing right here of the menace to physical health, nor to the malignant agencies that may be
hidden in these microscopic bacteria—these wandering
germinal entities, the central force of which is spirit;
may it not be concluded that chance, or will-impelled
vibrations may be the chariots by which they are borne
into the auras, the blood corpuscles and the convolutions of the brain, producing the most deleterious
effects upon the subject physically, mentally and morally. The clairvoyant eye perceives these effects and
unfleshed intelligences, pronounces them positive realities, though generally unknown to those whose range

of thought is interwoven into the materialistic objective rather than the higher subjective verities.

Writing of the great Positive Mind, the American
seer, Dr. A. J. Davis, recognizes the superiority, and
by inference, the eternity of spirit in these words:
"Spirit, the inmost and eternal, while the source of
power, is manifest in intellectual sensibility, the nerves
of affection and is the self-conscious volition of the
higher wisdom of faculties. . . . It is positively certain that the fixed affirmations of man's eternal spirit
are not the evanescent flames of a chemical battery,
nor are the social, moral and intellectual attributes of
man evolved from the physical basis of life. Grate-
fully I affirm that I have never been mis-impressed or
mis-educated enough to teach that man's intellectual
and spiritual nature was a product of the material
world. "

There is no crookedness in the above language. It
is clear and concise, and right the reverse of Haeckel
and such disciples of Darwin as those who teach that
man, physical, mental, moral and spiritual, sprang
up into being from matter and force—from apes and
orang-utangs.

At this point, without permission, I embody a portion of a letter written me by that superior sensitive
physician and exorcist, Dr. G. Lester Lane, of Boston,
Mass.:

". . . As you state, Doctor, in your communications,
every entity, atom, molecule and cell has within it a
central force, and evidently this force is a spirit-essence,
or substance, in some degree of refinement. . . .
In describing these entities, unseen by most eyes, I call
them spirit-atoms, or, in a sense, atomic conditions
which permeate the human body. Wherever there is

life, there is spirit, or God. And yet, my brother, I
stand ready today to proclaim without fear of contradiction from my enlightened teachers in spirit life,
that the spirit, or ego, or the central or soul-life,
though it be coated with material substance, does
enter into the nerve-centers of brain and body of
human beings now living; that these entities, or egos,
have once been the soul-centers or life of people who
have lived in the physical form *is a fact.* They are not
now in possession of that mortal body, but as entities
they are scattered through the human system and become a power sufficiently strong (when of a low order,
which they in most cases are) to absolutely and positively change that person's personality and desires to
such an extent that his life course, instead of being
upward, as designed by the Almighty, is downward.
They rob him of his characteristic personality and
deprive him of his self-respect. No matter what the
world may say to the contrary. I know—*positively
know—this to be a fact.* They, or many of them, are
the spirits of mortals who have once lived and walked
the earth as such. Being neither spiritually enlightened nor possessed of any desire for enlightenment,
they pass from the earthly tabernacle and enter the
lower spiritual zone where that same predominating
idea obtains as before. After a time retrogression sets
in and by virtue of magnetic and atmospheric currents
they drift about until coming in contact with a con-
genial aura they enter therein and become one of that
person's family, often numbering hundreds. Stagger-
ing, is it not? Yet, Doctor, it is true. They often exert
such a dominating influence over this person that they
actually compel him to eat food which they formerly
craved, thereby depraving his appetites as well as his
soul.

". . . Vague as this may seem to the casual observer, or the ordinary seer, I know that centuries hence it will be as an open book, for the people will have learned of the fact, the momentous fact of internal obsessions. . . . I am listening. . . .

"My spirit guide, Dr. Scott, says, 'Let me say a word.' "

" 'Greetings, brother in earth life!

" 'The greatest seers of the past were cognizant of the facts above stated, though crudely defined. By this knowledge they were enabled to penetrate the closely-drawn veil which seems to separate the material from the spiritual. What you call matter is barely observable by us, unless our attention is especially directed to it. We pass it, something as you pass through strata of fog. As you see leaves and straws floating in the atmosphere, so we see entities, emanations and spirit-centers of life and conscious forces surrounding you in your daily walks.

" 'Obsessions and possessions in a large degree dominate the thinking world today. History, it is said, often repeats itself. And certainly it is true of this newly-discovered fact: internal obsessions, which my medium has, while impressed by us, attempted to make more plain to you from our side of life.

" 'Centuries upon centuries ago people were as familiar with this so-called new discovery as the school children of today are familiar with primitive arithmetic and geography. There were great civilizations before the time of Babylon, before proud Greece or imperial Rome. So then, there's nothing new—at least in principle. Yet, we, dwelling in the spheres of immortality are controlling and representing the central guiding force of this medium; are determined that ere his exit from the mortal world this mammoth truth of *internal obsessions,* as well as the external shall be so put before the thinking, reasoning people as to be by them universally accepted.

" 'Turn your face once more toward this azure sky of enlightment, this mortal portal, and partake of such foods as we are anxious to give you. Come into our tent again. Partake of our spiritual bread and drink from our brimming cup. Come, and you shall go forth more fully equipped and inspirationally panoplied to do the Master's work.

" 'Peace and many years of health be unto you
in the flesh before you put off your sandals,
drop your pilgrim's staff and cross to our
side of the higher life.' "

(From spirit DR. SCOTT.)

Let us not forget that while thinking of matter, of oxygen, of hydrogen, or of any of the elements, that back of, or within the minutest atom or molecule of form there is substance, intelligence, energy; and that these molecules, entering the human system, must obsess, or influence, it just in the ratio of their psychic potency.

Scientists assure us that "electricity is constituted of corpuscles about one thirty-thousandth part of the size of the atoms of which all matter is composed, and these corpuscles are known to be the centers of force, free to move, and constituting, as they do, the life forces of the universe." As for the tremendous potency in these corpuscles, it is said that "two one-grain masses of corpuscles if placed four-tenths of an inch apart, the repulsion of each upon the other will be twenty quadrillions of a ton." Such mathematical estimates, strange indeed, may be set down as the miracles of science. And yet there are no miracles in the ecclesiastical sense of that word. As high an authority as Huxley wrote thus: "With regard to the miracle question, I can only say that the word *impossible* is not to my mind applicable to matters of philosophy. That the possibilities of nature are infinite is an aphorism with which I am wont to worry my friends."

It was the dictum of Farady that "all force allied to motion is will force." Even the vegetative diatomacea move about in all directions, supposedly by some such law as that which causes the ascension of the balloon, but I think rather by its inherent consciousness. Doubtless flowers are conscious on their plane of expression. I love them, and say in the silence, God beautify and bless you. Their central germs are entities. While I feel pulsing life all around me, I am not able to say there is no death. I pronounce that dead, judging by the sense-perceptions, which has no power to move—no power to produce itself—no power to cognize cause and effect—no power to select nutrition, nor has any aspiration to grow. The great granite boulder that capped the hillside back of the old school-house near the foot of the Green Mountains where I attended school over seventy-five years ago, remains there stationary, and if not dead, it is provokingly inactive. Those immense blocks of finely polished granite lining the King's Chamber in the great pyramid, have probably remained there for 5,000 years, and to the touch seemed cold and dead— dead as a mass. Prof. Lionele S. Beales, admittedly the greatest microscopist of the world, pronounced primordial matter dead—dead till force or combined

energizing forces infill and move it. But if dead to
the perceptions, life permeates it, for life—divine life
—pulses through all things, animate or inanimate—
and all life could come only from antecedent life.

It is stated, without contradiction, so far as I know,
that fourteen chemical elements enter into the composition of all the higher organized beings. There may
be more. These are carbon, oxygen, hydrogen, nitro-
gen, sulphur, phosphorus, chlorine, potassium, sodium,
calcium, magnesium, iron, fluorine and silicic acid. If
there are others they are not booked as actually demonstrated. And these above-named elements certainly
pre-existed in inorganic forms before being organized.
And organization biologically related to origin, differentiation, environing ether and those configurations of
outline that characterize entities and personalities,
physical, mental and moral, were surely impelled by
pre-existing forces. Pre-existence faces us, look which
way we will, and is equally as true on the psychic as
the physical plane of existence.

All, everything except Absolute Causation, manifest as cosmic consciousness, is subject to change—to
a perpetual flux, seen or unseen. The descending or
ascending circuit of force flows into and through every
electron, atom, cell and plant up to man. Force causes
motion, and "if motion could be arrested," says the
astronomer Flammarion, "if force could be destroyed,
if the temperature of the bodies could be reduced to
absolute zero, matter would cease to exist as we know;
but there would still be pre-existing substance."

"How can we reason," said Socrates, "but from
what we know." Hypotheses are cheap. Among the
things that we know is that man can throw off his over-
coat—throw off all his garments—and even his phys-

ical body by persistent fasting, becoming a mere shadow. And if so, why may he not as a spiritual being on another plane of conscious expression, throw off the sheathings of his particled soul-body, which has more attractions for the earthly than the spiritual, and consequently exist simply as a spirit-entity? And again, if man is a rational, moral actor—and he is—may he not hereafter disobey as well as obey law? If he may increase, may he not in manifestation decrease?

Do I hear—"Is not this a possible retrogradation?" Yes—and emphatically *no*, considering the all—the ONE. The sun retrogrades every autumn afar down the south-west skies, but it is not blotted out of existence. The parable-son went afar from home spending all that he had in "riotous living," went so deep into degradation that he would fain have filled himself with the "husks that the swine refused"—a terrible experience. But when he "came to himself"—when the spirit within awoke to conscious manliness, he said: "I will arise and go to my father." And mark—though he spent all that he had, he did not spend his conscious self—*his real atma*. So a spirit once incarnated in a mortal form and living a viciously selfish and depraved life—living solely for worldly and grossest ends, may continue this morally downward course in the invisible realms until he spends, disposes of his particled soul-form, he himself reverting to a prodigal spirit-entity.

Remember, reader, that while there are different grades of manifest matter interblending and shading into each other, something as do rainbow hues, there are also different degrees of radiant substances—differentiated atoms, and ether centers constituting the etheric soul-body. This, through the chemistry

pertaining to the lower spirit spheres, having during
the descending arc, dispersing and disposing of the
psychic or soul elements, becomes an individualized entity—that and nothing more—a wanderer on the earth-
plane of spirit existence, seeking some vortex of life,
some attracting aura, some inviting nerve-center, some
cranial convolution into which it may enter and dwell
as an influencing or obsessing influence—a very vam-
pire.

There are many mental phases and many occult
kinds of obsessions, those immediate and those
shadowy, subtle, invisible, forces from afar, and others
still that are simply self-induced hallucinations. In
my work entitled "Demonism of the Ages and Spirit
Obsessions" (page 199) I say:

"It must be considered that all obsessions are not
from surrounding unseen intelligences. There is a
sort of ideation obsession caused by an unbalanced,
weakened organization, and these are internal unbalanced forces. Everything objective and subjective
affects these persons. They are like tremulous aspens.
They are partly the victims of their own disordered
imaginations. They are emotional, suspicious, pessimistic sensationalists, touching the fringe-belt of morbidity, hearing the unheard, and seeing fanciful pictorial presentations, instead of genuine realities. This
sort of obsession is remedied by auto-suggestion, will
power, magnetic manipulation, and hypnotic treat-
ment scientifically administered."

CHAPTER V.

Long having wander'd since, round the earth having
    wander'd,
Now I face home again, very pleas'd and joyous.
(But where is what I started for so long ago?
And why is it yet unfound?)

I KNOW I am deathless.
I know that this orbit of mine cannot be swept by a
    carpenter's compass;
And whether I come to my own to-day, or in ten thou-
    sand or ten million years,
I can cheerfully take it now or with equal cheerfulness
    I can wait.   *—Whitman.*

The affirmation that whatever exists must exist
somewhere, requires no proof. A prophet of Israel
when wrapt in the ecstacy of inspiration exclaimed,
"The spirit is the candle of the Lord." The candle,
though located and stationary, floods with brightness
every portion of the apartment. And so the spirit,—a
flame of light—conscious and kingly, ensphered in a
golden ether circle, located in the coronal brain region,
illumines the whole physical and mental organization.

The segment tells prophetically of the circle, and
the cosmos, that measureless infinity of being, in its
unitive wholeness, is as rhythmic with music as are the
autumn-laden harvest fields when fanned by gentlest

breezes. If the blind and the deaf do not to-day sense the vibrations of this flow of music through this grand orchestra of nature, they will in the to-morrow of eternity. God's goodness is endless.

The falling leaves of dreary November decay—die to feed and nourish the trees and buds of spring. Under the compost the grass is greenest. As parts of the cosmos, the energies, elements and entities of skies and mountains, rocks, forests and flowers enter into our rude frame-works—our skeleton bodies, to obsess, lowering or lifting them to higher planes of realization.

Astronomers assure us that the interplanetary spaces, the vast ether-regions of our solar system, are crowded with flowing streams of meteoric fragments and fire-dust, which when drawn into our atmosphere flash and fall Vesuvius-like as ashes and unseen essences. It has been ''computed that more than 7,000,-000 of meteors fall nightly upon our earth, invisible or visible to the naked eye.'' If so, what countless millions of invisible fragments, what myriad hosts of meteoric bodies and detached life-entities may be floating about us, vitalizing, transforming, obsessing, and all to the non-clairvoyant eye unseen, unknown. Though one may feel to sing with the poet:

''I feel like one who treads alone
Some banquet hall deserted''—

no mortal is ever alone; unseen energies and entities, angelic or demoniac, attend all, doing their silent work according to atmospheric conditions, atomic environments and invisible vibrations, which impinge upon the enveloping auras of sensitives. This invisible network

—these aural emanations, are often broken into by disturbing, obsessing diakka.

Angels naturally abide in the etherial realms of ecstatic beauty and loveliness, passing to and from planetary worlds at will. And the more pure, exalted spirit intelligences undoubtedly dwell in the higher, clearer regions that obtain above us.

Mount Everest, a point of the Himalayas, is five and a half miles high. The highest inhabited place is Hanle in Thibet, 15,000 feet above the sea. Then comes San Vicente in the Bolivian Andes. At these altitudes the density of the air is only about one-half of the normal and the supply of oxygen is so insufficient that the people are frail and weakly. The higher the ascent up from the earth the colder the temperature and the greater the store of electricity. The Cirrus balloon of Berlin bearing a thermometer and barometer, upon reaching eleven and a half miles marked the temperature of 75 below zero. Our atmosphere is a fluid ocean extending off seventy-five or a hundred miles from our planet, and at that elevation all is pure as purity itself, befitting abode for the purer spirits— the seers and the adepts of the elder ages—if they so choose, or in the starry depths; while the lower, less unfolded spirits, the earth-bound, can no more rise to those lofty heights than fish can fly or lead float upon water. A law which may be termed spiritual attraction, as immutable as the law of gravity, holds them temporarily to the darker aerial zones that encircle our planet. Messages from them are often unreliable and never infallible. These earth-chained spirits, with innumerable entities, semi-conscious and conscious, dwell in the unclean, smokier localities that dot and darken so many of the dismal portions of our earth;

and they just as naturally obsess or cling to negative
sensitives as do bits of iron filings to magnets.

THE MONERON AND THE QUESTIONABLE ATOM.

The atom with its constituents is doubtless formed
from primary substance through the action and reac-
tion of magnetic and electro-chemical currents, the
mineral atom being qualitatively unlike that of the
vegetable. The latter from vibratory influx and internal differentiation is a grade higher in the line of evolution.

The lowest of all organized beings, the moneron, is
endowed with life and is a microscopal entity. It has
the powers of reproduction, and within its form is a
central force, or ruler. This ruler is sensitive, has the
power of determination and can move in a given
sphere independently. If divided into one or several
parts, there is influxed into each part the vital principle from the all-life, the Divine Presence. Each part
lives. Each part can procreate.

Just above the pre-existing moneron in the scale of
life, is found the amoeba. The higher is always based
upon the pre-existing lower, plus the addition of some
force or conscious substance. The amoeba has "a
central nucleous, the central intelligence of which,"
says Howard Cashmere, "controls the cell-body." And
this controlling force of the cell-body of all cells and
all cell formations, is spirit—or expressed in the plural,
infinitesimal spirits.

In treating of this central ruler, this conscious
entity, atma, ego, Thomson J. Hudson says:

"It has been variously designated as 'the vital principle,' the 'principle of life,' 'the soul,' 'the communal soul,' 'the supersensitive soul,' 'the spirit,' 'the unconscious mind,' 'the subconscious mind,' 'the subliminal consciousness,' 'the subjective mind' etc., the designation being governed by the point of view from which the subject is treated. But no one, be he materialist or spiritualist, denies its existence, or that it is endowed with an intelligence commensurate with the functions it performs in organic life. Philosophers may differ in their views as to its origin, or its ultimate destiny, or its psychological significance outside of the functions it performs in keeping the machinery of life in motion; but no one denies its existence, its intelligence, or its power over the functions, sensations and conditions of the body. . . .

"I point out the obvious truth that this central intelligence, operating upon the myriad intelligences of which the physical organism is composed, constitutes the mechanism, so to speak, by which the mind (the spirit) controls the body in health and disease."

But where, considering location, does this kingly ruler, the spirit, reign in the human organism?

Surely in the brain, rather than in the limbs or solar plexus. Sarcognomy, physiognomy, phrenology, and all the finer commanding forces, point to the coronal region of the brain as the necessary home of the spirit.

And "what the form and size of this conscious spirit, that intuitively knows, plans and wills?"

Only a materialist, unacquainted with the last words of scientific research, would propound such a question. Assuredly, it is not square nor trapezoidal in shape, nor is it, literally speaking, the size of a walnut or a mountain boulder. Some can only consider

5

refined substance, as avoirdupois, or as something akin
to the three visible dimensions of space. Worse than
this, they can think of spirit and its persisting energies, only in terms of matter.

It is pressingly asked, what then is—or what constitutes the human spirit?

Though measurably undefinable in language, it is
in our conception, an uncompounded, indivisible, particle of conscious life, encircled in a crystal-like aura
of dazzling brightness—a potentialized portion of the
Infinite, finited for the realization of manifestation on
the physical plane of mortality—the incarnate God
within us, which is the builder of the body and the commanding master of the innumerable cells, atoms and
electrons that constitute the human structure.

CHAPTER VI.

WHAT THE NATURE OF THE ATOM, AND DOES IT PRE-EXIST?

"Were once our beings blent and intertwining
And for that glory still my heart is pining;
Knew we the light of some refulgent sun
When once our souls were one?"

"Round us in waters of delight forever
Ravishingly flowed the heavenly nectar river;
We were the masters of the seal of things
And where truth in her everlasting springs
Quivered our glancing wings."
—*Schiller.*

Think, speculate as you may, O believer in the mind-and-force theory, that two human cells, mingling in darkness, with no purpose (or if any, with no higher purpose than sensual pleasure), could create a conscious rational spirit! Think of it in the line of geometrical ratios, mortality begetting, manufacturing immortality. Accept it, and you have an appalling mosaic miracle minus any God in the garden.

Do I hear that generation only evolves the spirit? But evolution implies substance to be evolved from, and whatever that substance or something was, it preceded—pre-existed; and so your own reasoning forces you to a belief in pre-existence.

Barely mentioning the Quadric of Von Staudt and the principle involved in the conic sections, it is enough to state that analytical geometry reveals and shows the enumeration and "perpetuation of constants," which may be thus summed up: that which, or whatever, thinks is potent; whoever thinks the thoughts of aspiration and purpose exists, pre-exists, before the thought.

It requires no argument to show that the atom with its dissociated fragments pre-existed before the molecule. But what is the "mighty atom," using the words of Marie Corelli, noted for her fine descriptions of social economy and her grasp of moral philosophy. We give you the best up-to-date statements of the world's most illustrious scientists and physicists, Prof. J. J. Thompson says he finds the atom to consist of a sphere of positive electricity within which are revolving, with enormous speeds, concentric rings of negative corpuscles, or electrons; the number of the latter being proportional to the atomic weight of the atom, and varying with different atoms from one thousand to two hundred and fifty thousand.

And Blondlot, writing of the N-rays, informs us "that by mathematical analysis and chemical mechanism, Thompson has had marvelous success in accounting for the known properties of various atoms, especially noteworthy being his explanations of the periodic law and of radio-activity."

Townsend of Oxford, to the same intent, informs us that the "part played by the positive electrons and ions in the genesis of the electrical spark, is of prime importance, giving us a clear picture of disunited atoms, and of the mechanism of the disruptive electrical discharges."

Those who have been building up pyramidal structures of force and matter out of atoms—atoms of matter, have been building upon the sand. The atom, so long pronounced indivisible, has gone, as an indivisible entity. It is literally abolished. In furtherance of this, at a late British association, Prof. Thompson and Lockyer both pronounced the atom to be complex and divisible. And Sir Oliver Lodge had previously declared that the "electrons, or natural electrical units, to be the ultimates behind the atom." And so scientists, physicists, after the profoundest of research, have united in the dethronement, destruction and burial of the once-pronounced "indivisible and mighty atom." But the electrons, divisible elements, and invisible entities, remain. There is no annihilation.

Do we—can we—begin to comprehend the heighth, the depth, the grandeur and the glory of this universe, pulsing with life and throbbing with activity? Imprisoned in the flesh, our dull ears cannot hear, and our dim eyes, unless in the ecstacy of independent clairvoyance, cannot see a millionth part of the world about us. If our inmost eyes were opened, we should behold cells, molecules, particles, electrons, entities, radiobes, spirit-centers of the minutest organisms,—whirling, dashing, in a seemingly purposeless profusion. Further, we could see the astral atmosphere, this surrounding realm of haze in which we live and move and breathe, filled with pre-existent spirit-germs of grasses, grains, buds, birds, animals and human spirits, non-incarnated; once incarnated nebulous groups, wild island tribes, races, nations, cities, temples of worshipers, restless politicians, churchianic hypocrites, psychic frauds, poor, frenzied millionaires just freed from their fleshly bodies, dazed and dimmed in vision— these latter wandering, fearing, hoping; recalling and recounting the deeds of their lives while vestured in earthly bodies, beginning now to fully realize that con-

science is the accuser, memory the undying worm, fame
and fashion, fossils; and "whatsoever a man soweth,
that shall he reap." There is no possible escape. God
is just.

THE ORIGIN OF THE HUMAN SPIRIT.

It had no origin—none except in manifestation.
Creation must not be confounded with evolution nor
with objective realization.

While it is conceded that atoms, electrons and radiobes have individualized forms and polarities, with
forces attractive and repellent, they are not creative.
The spark from frictioned flint and steel is simply
evolved from what was previously involved therein.
The basis of evolution is involution. Water does not
flow from a dry fountain, and all loud prating of evolution—virtually evolution from nothing—is but child-
ish prattle.

In the dry, shell-incrusted acorn there abides the
involved pre-existing life-germ, from which, when
given soil, moisture and warmth, there is evolved the
towering oak. The simile of flint and steel as related
illustratively to the human spirit shows in manifestation that the germinal life-principle involved in the
spermatazoa, uniting magnetically with the life elements of the negative ovum, evolves—that is, affords
the conditions for the pre-existing spirit's implantation and manifestation upon this mortal plane of existence.

Possibly afire with the intensity of conviction, I may
be spirit-mad; but I insist that that expression of energy
which we call spirit, and which moulds the various
elements into living forms and endows organisms with

the functions of nutrition, growth, reproduction, and still upward with consciousness, the faculties of thought, and intellectual aspirations, is spirit—Conscious, Potent Spirit, and that this spirit pre-existed as the formative life-principle.

CHAPTER VII.

———

"Of the beginning that never began is life's tale,
And that never-finishing ending to which we all
    sail—
For the children of never and ever we are,
And our home is beyond, and our goal is afar."

Contrasted with stoicism in its naked stolidity—
contrasted with the teachings of the laughing Democri-
tus, the weeping Hieraclitus, and the materialistic Epi-
curus and other cold, inductive sophists who considered matter and unreasoning force—the only force
that causes water to run into frost-forms upon window-
panes—we turn with delight to Plato and Socrates,
Proclus and Jesus, Swedenborg and Hugo, Emerson
and Davis, and S. J. Finney, and other great, inspired
souls standing in brightness upon the mount of
vision—souls regenerated and so illumined that they
saw a universe afire with purpose and aflame with
essential spirit—the equivalent of a guiding, molding
Intelligence. Swedenborg declares that "there is one
sole Essence, one sole Substance, and one sole Form,
the Divine, from which are all essences, substances and
forms that are created." Hegel teaches that "the
substratum underlying all phenomenal existence is
God, the Infinite Being."

The deductive thinker, Selden J. Finney, one of the
most brilliant minds ever in the ranks of Spiritualists,
observed that:

72

"If infinite mind evolved the physical universe, then mind first became body. If mind becomes body, form 'matter,' it must do so by descent, precipitation, condensation. . . . Infinite mind descends into 'creation,' its body and chronology, only by approximate materialization. The two processes are equivalent and correlative,"—pre-exisiting and existing.

Dana, the great geologist and mineralogist, says this in the "American Journal of Science and Arts:"

"For the development of man gifted with high reason and will, and thus made a power above material nature, there was required, as Alfred R. Wallace has urged, a special act of a Being above nature, whose Supreme Will is not only the source of natural law, but the working-force of nature herself,—this I still hold."

It is the spirit that constitutes the man, and finite man bears a similar relation to God, the Infinite Spirituality, that a crystal drop bears to a perpetual fountain. This is the root-thought of pre-existence.

It is very clear to profound thinkers that once in existence as *divine man, always* in existence. The converse is equally true; once absolutely *out* of existence, never *in* existence! This logical bulwark has never been successfully assailed and overthrown by materialists.

In the phrase, "once *in* existence, always in existence," I am referring to conscious, to *divine man,* and not to sticks and stones, nor to stinging insects. These are fragments—imperfect structures—unfinished temples. And no one gifted with intelligence speaks of a conscious rock, a divine wolf, or a righteous dog. These are not, and never were, in existence as consciously rational and morally progressive beings. They have not the Spiritual Keystone. They are not religious; neither are they conscious of their subordinate consciousness! And certainly no logician ever affirms of a part what he does of *a whole*. A slice slashed from a golden orange, thin, irregular, ill-shapen and seedless, is not equal to nor should it be compared with the well-rounded orange. Vile, vicious animals, serpents, spiders and noxious insects are but parts, bearing the same relation to *man* that passing thoughts bear to permanent ideas, or shadows to substances. Carnivorous animals and insects are never in existence as perfect structures, as *divine entities;* but rather as fleeting organisms serving temporary uses. Yet, the higher order of animals, humanly magnetized, may exist hereafter. They doubtless do.

The problem of pre-existence is included in the provinces of mental science, metaphysics and religion, rather than in that of the physical sciences. Science may afford important aid by revealing the laws of movement; but its sphere being limited to the *order* and *sequence* of phenomena, it can never reveal the inner nature of things in themselves.

Many of the most enlightened minds of all ages and countries have taught that man's conscious self-hood is as much a matter of the past as it is to be of the future. The proofs of this rest more upon axioms, intuitions, spiritual cognitions, direct revelations from angels and exalted spirits, prophets and poets and the seers of the ages, than upon evidence directed to or proceeding from the perceptive senses, or to the didactic faculty.

An eminent English writer remarks: "This doctrine of pre-existence in some of its different forms, was at one time the doctrine taught in the Divine Apocalypse, in the books of Enoch, and Fohi, in Bhaga-Vad Gita, in the teachings of the Celtic Druids, and in the lore of the old Babylonians and Egyptians."

Pythagoras, the founder of the Italic school of Greek philosophy, not only taught pre-existence, but professed to have a distinct remembrance of it.

Plato believed that all the knowledge of laws and principles we acquire in this world is simply a recovery of reminiscence of knowledge which the soul possessed in a previous state of existence. Readers of Plato will remember the reference to " Meno," where Plato introduces Socrates as making an experiment, by way of putting a series of questions to a slave of Meno, eliciting from the uneducated youth geometrical truths. This done, Socrates triumphantly observed to Meno, "I have not taught the youth anything; but simply interrogating him, he recalled the knowledge he had in a previous existence." Plato further taught that all ideas, types, and ultimate forms both precede and succeed their material embodiments.

Ammonius Saccas, founder of that school of eclectic philosophy known as New Platonism, and among whose disciples were Longinus and Origen, was a believer in pre-existence.

Plotinus, an eminent Greek philosopher, an adept in the doctrines of the Oriental sages, and a teacher of philosophy at Rome from 245 A. D. until his death, was an advocate of pre-existence.

Proclus, a student of Olympiodorus, at Alexandria, and for a time at the head of the New Platonic schools, believed in pre-existence.

Appollonius, of Tyanna, a Pythagorean philosopher of the first century, venerated for his wisdom by his contemporaries, and whose thrillingly interesting life was written by Flavius Philostratus, was a believer in and teacher of pre-existence.

Leibnitz, the most profound philosopher of the

seventeenth century, held the doctrine of pre-existence as one of his cardinal beliefs.

Sir Walter Scott makes this observation: "How often do we find ourselves in society which we have never before met, and yet feel impressed with a mysterious and ill-defined consciousness that neither the scene, the speakers, nor the subject are entirely new; nay, feel as if we could anticipate that part of the conversation which has not yet taken place!"

In his diary he further said: "I cannot, I am sure, tell if it is worth marking down, that yesterday, at dinner-time, I was strongly haunted by what I would call the sense of pre-existence, in a confirmed idea that nothing which passed was said for the first time; that the same topics had been discussed, and the same persons had stated the same opinions on them. . . . The sensation was so strong as to resemble what is called *mirage* in the desert, or a calenture on board a ship. . . . It was very distressing yesterday, and brought to my mind the fancies of Bishop Berkeley about an ideal world."

Sir S. C. Groom Napier, one of England's cleverest thinkers, was as firm an advocate of pre-existence as were Charles and Edward Beecher of America.

Plato emphatically declares—"Our soul was something before it came to exist in this present human form, whence it appears to be immortal, and as such it will subsist for ever after death."

Empedocles, cherishing opinions similar to Plato's, assures us that—"There is no production, or anything, which was not before; no new substance made which did not really pre-exist; therefore, in the generations and corruptions of inanimate bodies, there is no form or quality really distinct from the substance produced and destroyed, but only a various composition and modification of matter. But in the generation and corruption of men, where the souls are substances really distinct from the matter, there is nothing but the conjunction and separation of souls, and particular bodies existing, both before and after; not the production of any new soul into being, which was not before, nor the absolute death, and destruction of anything into nothing.''

Poets and prophets, being inspired, they get down to the very soul of realities, and I am proud to state that the world's great poets as well as the most highly-illumined Spiritualists of the ages, have believed and taught the doctrine of pre-existence. Here I use Spiritualists and Spiritualism as the direct antitheses of materialists and materialism.

"Though descending from realms divine,
 We must drink the cup of sorrow deep
 Ere we can comfort anyone's distress;
 For, from the heart bruised by a thousand ills,
 The tears if sympathy alone can flow.

Our home is the land of day,
 Our journeying is all that way;
 Our love is in God's paradise.''
                              —*James Macbeth Bain.*

CHAPTER VIII.

Trismegistus! three times greatest!
   How the name sublime
Has descended to this latest
   Progeny of time!

By the Nile I see him wandering,
   Pausing now and then,
On the mystic union pondering
Between gods and men;
Half-believing, wholly feeling,
   With supreme delight,
How the gods, themselves concealing,
   Lift men to their height.

Or in Thebes, the hundred-gated
   In the thoroughfare
Breathing, as if consecrated,
   A diviner air;
And amid discordant noises,
   In the jostling throng,
Hearing far, celestial voices
   Of Olympian song.

Who shall call his dreams fallacious?
   Who has searched or sought
All the unexplored and spacious
   Universe of thought?
Who, in his own skill confiding,
   Shall with rule and line
Mark the borderland dividing
   Human—and divine?

                    Longfellow.

Personality in its common and outward acceptation is usually associated with appearance and outward character; but with such writers as Emerson, James Freeman Clarke, Frohschammer, Elisha Mulford, Lotze, etc., personality has a far deeper meaning. The Latins used *Persona* to signify personating, counterfeiting, or wearing a mask. But personality in the sense in which Emerson employs it signifies true being, both concrete and spiritual. It alone is original being. It is not limited. Personality is that universal element that pervades every human soul, and which is at once its continent and ground of being. Distinction from others and limitation by them results from Individuality, not the inmost Personality.

Elisha Mulford says: "There is in conscious personality the highest that is within the knowledge of man. It is the steepest, loftiest summit toward which we move in our attainment."

Emerson says: "The personal within man is the soul of the whole; the wise silence; the universal beauty, to which every part and particle is equally related. . . . The personal is not an organ, not a function, not a faculty; it is the background of our being—an immensity not possessed and that cannot be possessed."

We are here again brought back to what was said above, that all spirits cohere in one social solidarity by virtue of the principle of Love which inheres alike in each. Personality, therefore, pertains to "the substance of the spirit and individuality to its form." Others reverse these words. Individuality, rooted in spirit, is the far greater word. Unfolding and widening, it becomes unmeasurable in magnitude and irresistible in force.

PHILOSOPHERS WHO TAUGHT PRE-EXISTENCE.

The Magi of Persia, the Hierophants of Egypt, the Brahmins of India, and Buddhists of the East, each and all held to some form of the general doctrine. Jesus recognized his own pre-existence when he spoke of the "glory He had with the Father before the world was." Again He said: "Before Abraham was, I am;" that is to say, before Abraham was in the physical expression, I existed as a spirit. Many of the most enlightened minds of all countries have taught that man's conscious selfhood is as much a matter of the past as it is to be of the future.

"Our soul," says Plato, "is a particle of the Divine Breath, and therefore we are related to God. Our spirit's divine ideas are natural and are created by the contemplation of divine things. Before it was associated with the body, it existed in God; even now, though enveloped by the body, it may participate in that divine contemplation through the subjection of the passions, and through a contemplative life."

In the song of Amosis we read: "Lord, thou hast been our dwelling place in all generations; before the mountains were brought forth, or ever thou hadst formed the earth and the world."

The most learned among the Christian fathers, such as Origen, accepted the doctrine of pre-existence.

Jerome of 340 A. D., said of the doctrine of re-incarnation which prevailed in India and Egypt: "This wicked and impious doctrine was anciently diffused through Egypt and the East, and now prevails in secret, as in vipers' nests, among most, and pollutes the purity of those regions; and as by a hereditary disease glides in the few to pervade the many."

Clemens of Alexandria, in his Eclogues, advocated the soul's pre-existence, but stoutly denied the doctrine of reincarnation—and the reincarnation of human souls. He contended that the passage: "There was a man sent from God" meant that the soul of John the Baptist was older than his body, and was sent from his former state.

Clement of the second century, educated in the Platonic philosophy, and afterwards a disciple of Pantenus in Alexandria, said: "Do we not love God this first, that we exist, that we are said to be men? That descending from the regions of light, or sent by Him, we are held in these corporeal bodies."

Pamphilas, who established a flourishing school in Caesarea, who vindicated Origen in five books, and was martyred 309 A. D., was a strong advocate of the soul's pre-existence. "Does matter create the soul?" he asked. "The house resembles the idea that preceded it, and the entrance by a path from the mountains resembles the descent of souls from Heaven to their lodgment in bodies."

Synesius, a Neo-Platonic philosopher and disciple of Hypatia at Alexandria, wrote largely in favor of pre-existence. When the citizens of Ptolemais had invited him to the bishopric among them, he declined that dignity, in a letter to his brother on the subject, for this reason among others, that he cherished certain opinions which perhaps all would not approve, but which he could in no wise abjure, as after mature reflections they had struck their roots deep in his mind. First among these he mentioned the doctrine of pre-existence. "Assuredly I can never think it right to believe the soul an after-birth of the body." Vestiges of this belief are openly discernible in his writings, as,

6

for example, in the hymn of which the following is a
paraphrase:

> "Eternal Mind, thy seedling spark
> Through this thin vase of clay,
> Athwart the waves of chaos dark
> Emits a timorous ray!
>
> Far forth from *thee,* thou central fire,
> To earth's sad bondage cast,
> Let not the trembling spark expire—
> Absorb thine own at last!"

The doctrine of the spirit's pre-existence was held
by the Jews, both before and contemporary with the
Apostolic period. It was certainly held by the later
Jews living after the times of the Babylonish captivity.
Among their proofs they quote this from the Book of
Wisdom:

"I was an ingenuous child, and received a good
soul; nay more, being good, I came into a body undefiled."

Writing of the Essenes, Josephus says: "For the
opinion obtains among them (the Essenes) that bodies
indeed are corruptible, and the matter of them not permanent; but that spirits continue exempt from death
forever; and that, emanating from the most subtle
ether, they are enfolded in bodies, as prisons, to which
they are drawn by some natural spell. But when loos-
ened from the bonds of the flesh, as if released from a
long captivity, they rejoice and are borne upward. . . .
This company of disembodied spirits is distributed in
different orders. The law of some of them is to enter
mortal bodies, and, after certain prescribed periods,

be again set free. But those possessed of a diviner structure are absolved from all local bonds of earth.''

Today, in the full blaze of scientific discovery, there are hosts of men famous for their knowledge of the sciences, who believe in a pre-existent state of conscious existence. Among these are Prof. Redfield, the author and distinguished physiognomist; Charles and Edward Beecher, lately departed to the higher life; G. Groom Napier and Sir Thompson of England.

Nearly the whole body of French philosophers of psychic studies, including such men as Figuer and Camille Flammarion, the astronomer, hold to the doctrine of pre-existence. The great Fourier taught it. All the religionists of the Orient did, and to a very large extent the literati of Continental Europe accept it today.

WHAT EXALTED SPIRITS SAY OF PRE-EXISTENCE.

Conscious communion with spirits, while not proving immortality in the sense of endless existence, does prove a conscious existence after death. And then, those long inhabiting the better realms of angelic blessedness—that is to say, ancient spirits—almost uniformly teach pre-existence. I cannot this moment call to mind a case to the contrary. It is admitted, however, that spirits of the spirit-world differ upon this subject; and further, that testimony of spirits is authoritative only so far as it corresponds with intuition and the highest reason. Truth is the only final authority. Still, the persistence of an idea and the potency of intelligent majorities necessarily influence convictions. And I am certain that the general tenor of the teachings of wise and highly intelligent spirits upon this subject favors a pre-existent state of being. Aaron Knight, two hundred years in spirit life, and whose identity I took the pains to establish when in England several years since, teaches, with the "brotherhood of ancient sages," pre-existence in the most positive manner.

Divinity is eternal. An essential man is constituted, according to Plato, of divine substance, form and germ; and further, with this prince of thinkers, essential forms, types and ideas, were the same. Types, or ideas, in fact, were subjective realities. Outworked they became partially visible. Still, the type preceded and succeeded the visible appearance. The material contents of form as in the oak or animal, are fleeting, changing; but the hidden essential form, which is the type, or idea, is enduring and immortal.

Every argument against pre-existence, is so far as entitled to the name, an argument against the immortality of the spirit and a help to cold, controversial materialists. And materialism, in its last analysis, amounts to this—a whining puppy and a royal-souled prince; a beef-steak and a Lord Bacon, were all the same originally — fire-dust — atoms— protoplasmic atoms, adjusted and arranged for specific aims and ends by non-designed and non-intellectual molecular force. And so all conscious life—all noble aspirations for eternal unfoldment—automatically begin and necessarily end, in matter. Causation and matter are not equivalents. A stream cannot rise above its fountain. Thank God and the wisdom angels, Spiritualism and Theosophy in connection with the rational doctrine of pre-existence, save from this dreary slough of hopeless despondence.

If the sum total constituting that distinguished scientist, Lord Kelvin, were once absolutely out of existence, putting him into existence would be equivalent to creating something from nothing—a momentous miracle! As a thinker, I am a firm, undaunted believer in the spirit's pre-existence. The theory is the rational stronghold of the spirit's immortality. But pre-existence and reincarnation are by no means identical; they are not predicated and grounded upon the same philosophical basis; and yet, they relate to the continuity of life, the latter implying the rotation of life upon the wheel of a merciless fate until Nirvana, whatever that may be, is attained. Writers who confound the above exhibit a painful non-acquaintance with the meaning of language.

That there is an underlying truth, however, in the theory of reincarnation, few with a philosophic turn of mind will deny, but not as taught in the old oriental books—taught as the equivalent of transmigration, that is, the return of human spirits back, to be re-born into lizards, serpents, jackals and various brutes. Intelligent spirit-hood re-born into brute-hood is not in consonance with the great law of evolution, which indicates the upward tendency of all things. But reincarnation considered in relation to involution and as the descending arc of the circle, is not only plausible but logically true. And so I am a believer in re-incarnation in the higher esoteric sense of that all-too-often misunderstood principle.

Only the few can clearly recall events and experiences occurring in a previous state of being. Many did, however, in the more meditative past. And some in the present can do this; and their testimony upon the point is direct and positive. I have space to name but a few.

Judge Boardman, well known in Wisconsin for many years as a thoughtful, influential Spiritualist, repeatedly assured me that he could distinctly remember many things that transpired in his pre-existent life.

Judge Elliott, quite as much a mathematician as jurist, used to interest his friends by similar direct statements.

Harold Harrin, the Polish scholar, author and personal friend of Dr. Redfield, the New York physiognomist, often affirmed in the most positive manner, that he could remember many acts and events occurring in his pre-existent home in the heavens. Others testify to the same facts. Pre-existence is to them positive knowledge. Negative testimony upon this subject is of little account. That blind men do not see the sun is their misfortune—nothing more.

"A gentle strain of music," says Charles Dickens— "or the rippling of water in a silent place, or the odor of a flower, or even the mention of a familiar word, will sometimes call up sudden dim remembrances of scenes that never were in this life; which vanish like a breath; which some brief memory of a happier existence long gone by, seemed to have awakened."

Often in more thoughtful hours, contemplating upon spirit existence, have I felt that poets were not only inspired, as were those of Israel and Assyria, those like Dante and Poe, Tennyson and Longfellow, but that their creations were burning efforts to quench an immortal thirst. The object of pure poetry is beauty combined with a prophecy of the truth that is to be. It touches the heart-strings of the skies, and rebounding thrills the heart-strings of humanity. All great poets, rising up onto the moral altitude of the cosmic consciousness, tasting the delicious fruits of divinity,

have sung of pre-existence, and of the meetings somewhere and sometime of mated spirits—mating and
blending into one never-ending parting of love and
wisdom. To this end, Edwin Markham sings:

I.

"It was ages ago in life's first wonder
    I found you, Virgilia, wild sea-heart;
And 'twas ages ago that we went asunder,
    Ages and worlds apart.

"Your lightsome laugh and your hair's dark glory,
    I knew them of old by an ocean-stream,
In a far, first world, now turned to story,
    Now faded back to dream.

"I saw you there with the sea-girls fleeing,
    And I followed fast over rock and reef,
And you sent a sea-fire into my being,
    The lure of the lyric grief.

.   .   .   .

"I followed you fast through the white sea splendor,
    On into the rush of a blown, black rain;
Drawn on by that mystery strangely tender,
    The lure of the lyric pain.

"As up around the headlands the tides came hurling,
    You sang one song from your wild sea-heart;
Then a mist swept in, and we two went whirling,
    Ages and worlds apart.

II.

"We are caught in the coil of a world's romances—
    We come from high worlds and we go afar;
I have missed you again in the Earth's wild
        Chances—
    Now to another star.

"Perhaps we are led and our loves are fated,
  And our steps are counted one by one;
Perhaps we shall meet and our souls be mated,
  After the burnt-out sun.

"For over the world a dim hope hovers,
  The hope at the heart of all our songs—
That the banded stars are in league with lovers,
  And fight against their wrongs.

"If this all is a dream, then perhaps our dreaming
  Can touch life's height to a finer fire;
Who knows but the heavens and all their seeming
  Were made by the heart's desire?

"One thing shines clear in the heart's sweet reason,
  One lightning over the chasm runs—
That to turn from love is the world's one treason
  That treads down all the suns.

"So I go to the long adventure, lifting
  My face to the far, mysterious goals,
To the last assize, to the final sifting
  Of gods and stars and souls.

. . . .

III.

"There are more lives yet, there are more worlds
      waiting,
  For the way climbs up to the eldest sun,
Where the white ones go to their mystic mating,
  And the Holy Will is done.

"I will find you there where our low life heightens—
  Where the door of the wonder again unbars,
Where the old love lures and the old fire whitens,
  In the Stars, behind the stars.

. . . .

"Ah, strangely then will the heart be shaken,
  For something starry will touch the hour;
And the mystic winds of the worlds will waken,
  Stirring the soul's tall flower.

"As we go star-stilled in the mystic garden,
  All the prose of this life-run there to rhyme,
How eagerly will the poor heart pardon
  All of these hurts of Time!

"For 'twill all come back—the wasted splendor,
  The heart's lost youth like a breaking flower,
The dauntless dare, and the wistful, tender
  Touch of the golden hour."

CHAPTER IX.

———

"He, too, is there; and can we dream
    Their joy is other now than when
They dwelt among the sons of God,
    As walking in the eternal gleam?"
.   .   .   .
"Our little systems have their day;
    They have their day and cease to be;
They are but broken lights of thee,
    And thou, O Lord, are more than they."
.   .   .   .

Among the classical authors and noted characters referred to in the early Christian era, were Cerinthus, Celsus and Lucian, all opposed to the Christian religion in all or some of its more dogmatic features. These noted persons are named because they lived in the first and second centuries, engaging in the triangular controversies of Christianity—Jewish, Pagan and Churchianic—and are reported to have been believers in the spirit's eternal past pre-existence.

Origen's exhaustive reply to the clever skeptic and epicurean philosopher, Celsus, filled several volumes, the under-current being an effort to harmonize Christianity and Platonism. Some of the arguments of this illustrious Greek, criticizing church dogmas, were not fully met by this eminent Christian father (born A. D. 186), one of which was the atonement by substitution, a relic of Babylonian blood-shedding filtered down through Jewish teachings, and culminating in these words ascribed to Paul: "Without the shedding of blood there's no remission of sin." Sin is self-convicting and self-retributing. All wrong-doing meets with a just recompense. The scales must balance. Equity is the purpose of divine law; punishment, wrongly named, being disciplinary and amendatory. If justice in the line of cause and effect lifts the rod, wisdom directs the blow, and mercy—tender and loving —holds the balm to heal the wound, and the Christ-spirit is there to illumine and lead the penitent up to loftier heights.

Among his dialogues nothing is more instructingly amusing and historically interesting than his sale of the philosophers, and in the sale by the gods Lucian's religious convictions came to the surface.

After selecting and installing the philosopher of his and past periods in the slave-mart, he calls upon the gods, Mercury and Jupiter, to bid them off. The time having arrived, Mercury commands Jupiter to begin at once.

Merc. Whom shall we put upon the block first?

Jup. This fellow with the long hair—the Ionian— he is rather an imposing personage. He must sell well.

Merc. You, Pythagoras! step out and up and show thyself to the company. . . . Gentlemen, we here offer you a professor of the very best and most select description—who buys? Who wants a choice cut above the rest of the world? Who wants to understand the harmonies of the universe? and how to live two lives?

Customer (turning the philosopher around, looking at him, and giving him a slap on the back). He is not bad to look at. What can he do? What does he know best?

Merc. Arithmetic, astronomy, prognostics, geometry, music, conjuring—you've a first-rate sooth-sayer before you, one that can converse with the gods and foretell the future.

Cust. May one ask him a few questions?

Merc. Certainly—and much good may the answers do you.

Here follow the answers to several questions put to Pythagoras by those who thought of purchasing him, relating to his birthplace, his education, his travels, his beliefs concerning God, pre-existence and reincarnation.

"I was born in the isle of Samos; was educated in Egypt among the priests in their temples and the wise men living there. I devoted my time to the study of numbers, hearing and being taught; to travel in different lands—to research into nature's secrets—to many fastings—to periods of silence—to the evening baths—to the avoidance of animal flesh-eating—to the worship of the gods at the rising of the sun—to the singing of a hymn before meals—to the enjoying of celibacy—to the wearing of white garments—and to the purifying of the thoughts and deeds as a prelude to mystic associations with the gods in dreams and visions."

Cust. Suppose I buy you now. What will you teach me?

Pyth. I will teach you nothing—only recall things to your memory. . . . (All knowledge is but "recollection"—is a teaching ascribed to Pythagoras, Plato and other sages of antiquity.)

Cust. Then how will you teach me to recall things to my memory?

Pyth. First, I will cleanse and properly direct your thoughts, then purify your mind and wash away all the rubbish that has become attached to you—and then will ask you to go into repose and silence. After your period of silence you may begin the study of music, numbers, the nature of earth and air, fire and water, then motions and what caused their forces.

Pythagoras, a great personality, was a son of the god Apollo, being spiritually overshadowed at the conception something as was Jesus of the New Testament.

Jamblichus wrote: "No one can doubt that the spirit of Pythagoras was sent to mankind from the empire of the god of Wisdom, Apollo being either an attendant on the god, or co-arranged with him in some other more familiar way. This may be inferred from his birth and the all-various wisdom of his soul."

The Pythian oracle at Delphi foretold his birth—a gift divine to earth, an illustrious prerogative, surpassing in beauty and wisdom all who had ever lived before, because of his pre-existent state and because his birth had been predicted by the Pythian oracle.

As a traveler, he spent twenty-two years in Egypt, meeting the priests in the Adyta and in their temples. Later he was taken captive by Cambysis' soldiers and carried to Babylon, forming a friendship with the Magi, studying astronomy, music and mathematics. After remaining twelve years with these Magi he returned to Samos, establishing a school known as the "*semi-circle of Pythagoras.*" In this school of wisdom he taught hygiene, the divine mysteries, the soul's pre-existences, the method of converse with the gods, the holding of all things in common, the rejection of animal flesh-eating, the law of harmony and purity of life as the prelude to vision and prophecy. His communistic family-school numbered at one time six hundred, and from it there went out much of the thought and the wisdom that has flashed in broken lights down through all the ages. If he were in bodily form today he would be found with the Shakers at Mt. Lebanon, New York.

Cust. A queer idea that one must become a fiddler and learn geometry before he can be accounted a wise man.

Pyth. Though queer it is true—and assuredly, music, numbers, earth and air have form, for there could be no motion manifest without form. Besides, you shall learn that Deity consists of Mind, Number and Harmony.

Cust. What you say is really wonderful.

Pyth. Besides what I have just told you, you shall understand that you, yourself, who seem to be one individual, are really somebody else.

Cust. Do you mean to say I'm somebody else, and not myself, talking to you?

Pyth. Just at this moment you are; but you lived before this life, and upon another time you appeared in another body and under another name; and hereafter you will pass into another form still.

It is reported of Pythagoras that he professed to be conscious of having been formerly Euphorbus, one of the chiefs present at the siege of Troy, and of subsequently having borne other shapes and names. There is also a legend of his having interfered on behalf of a dog which was being cruelly beaten, declaring that in its cries he recognized "the voice of a departed friend." Be this a myth and nothing more, it tends to incite kindness to the helpless animals that look up to and trust us.

The above dialogue is introduced to show that the spirit's pre-existence was an almost universal belief among the philosophers of Greece and Rome in their palmiest periods. And it was emphatically taught by the great Galilean Rabbi. These are among his teachings:

"For thou didst love me before the foundations of the world."

"O Father, glorify thou me with thine own self with the glory which I had with thee before the world was."

"I come forth from the Father and am come unto the world; again I leave the world and go to my Father."

Conversing once with a most exalted spirit, properly an angel from the Christ-heavens, upon the origin of the human spirit, he replied with great emphasis: "It had no origin, unless descent and manifestation on the material plane of life is origin. It is not strange that individuals in whom intellect predominates over intuition and spirituality, should utterly ignore the spirit's pre-existence. But which is first, the musician or the harp? the imposing palace or the architect? the earthly fleeting body or the spirit? The truth upon this subject as taught in our spiritual heaven is this: The spirit, allied to God as is light to the sun of your planet, is the conscious intelligence—the enthroned life; and descending and incarnating for some good purpose, builds its earthly habitation from the germ-principle conditioned by generation. It can live without a human body, for it existed prior to it. It entered into it at will and can leave it when rightly conditioned previous to the complete separation and transition. We see such disembodied spirits in the spheres of the underworld. Some of these return to their own bodies—wiser for their research, while others entering the auras and organizations of negative persons, infest at first, then after a time *obsess* them. To us your world is the earthland of darkness, and the most of you seem to us like children struggling for selfish mastery. Your fleshly bodies serve you well for a season, as do the husks the corn, the chaff the wheat; but the death-angel later removes the fleshly rag and lets the prisoner free.''

A distinguished English writer, exhuming from the dust of the ages an important document ascribed to Enoch, gives us this valuable gem:

''Prepare thy spirit for its future existence,
When it hath awakened from the swoon of mortality;
These things did he show me,
That Angel of the Lord of Splendors;
The institution of heaven in the heavens,
And in the worlds that are under the heavens,
The spirits that delight in each, abide in each,
Till they descend to take the mortal form.''

CHAPTER X.

———

"God is a worker. He has thickly strewn
Infinity with grandeur. God is love,
He yet shall wipe away *creation's tears,*
And *all the worlds shall* summer in his smile."
                    —*Alexander Smith.*

Though pre-existence and reincarnation are not exact equivalents, nor are they necessarily connected, yet they bear much of the relation to each other that life today bears to life tomorrow—that the continuity of life bears to eternity. Accordingly, we here present the re-incarnation side of this question in full as taught in its highest and also lowest phases—oriental and occidental.

"And in that far off time
Thou shalt be I;—when I am cold and dead,
Thou shalt take up again life's silver thread.
If so, I charge thee hearken to my warning;
For I have somehow missed the goal in life.

But thou, my other self, may'st profit
By these my failures in its war and strife.
The separate goal,—the personal salvation,
Must seem a selfish end in thy new eyes.
Humanity's great soul be thy soul,
To perish with it, or with it to rise.
For when thou wakest, I shall be forgotten,

> And thou shalt get thee coats of skin again,
> And joy in life with all its glorious newness,
> Unconscious of this life's grief or pain.
> Ah, well! I merge my hopes and aspirations
> In thee; and I will henceforth bring to thee
> The sacrifice of all my lower nature,
> That thou may'st rise unfettered, fearless, free.
> Perhaps the one supreme initial effort,
> The choice between the evil and the good,
> That made thee possible, is marked by foot-
>   prints,
> Where my thorn-torn and bleeding feet have
>   trod.''

The descendants of the Epigoni are not yet extinct. They linger always dying, yet never quite dead. They revolve in a circle, selfishness being the attractive center. They seek the rest that rusts, while the inspired, standing high upon the mountain tops of vision, live and move above the haze-tinged clouds of prejudice and all narrow-mindedness. They come down from their towering heights as necessity requires, to tell their visions, plant the seeds of progress, then returning to their aerie heights for meditation and further, deeper spiritual unfoldment. Praying in secret, kneeling at the shrine of silence, they are in fellowship with the gods.

The wise learn from the mistakes they make. There is no inconsistency in changing opinions—in changing for the better. Goethe said inability to change meant a devitalized or dead mind. The growing mind needs change. The privilege to change is implied in the right to free action, which in its turn implies the right to correct all errors.

Inspiration lifting the veil, shows that aspiration is the measure of destination, and holds up in clearest light the balance of involution and evolution—the two halves of the circle of being.

We present first what may be termed the eclipse, the dark side of the reincarnation theory. Be not dismayed at these lower levels. When the sun is rising the shadow precedes the substance.

An Indian poet expresses his feelings upon the re-embodiment or reincarnation in the following words:

"How many births have passed, I cannot tell,
How many yet to come, no man can say;
But this alone I know, and know full well,
That pain and grief embitter all the way."

Upon the published authority of Mrs. Besant, one of our brilliant adepts in theosophy, Madame Blavatsky, very soon after her departure by death, was reincarnated, entering into the healthy, vigorous body of a young Hindu of India. In consonance with this teaching, the following dialogue was printed in the "Diary Leaves" of the "Theosophist," by J. S. Olcott in 1895. The subject was: "Transmigration, Reincarnation, and the Power of the Yogi to Re-Embody:"

"Question. Up to what day, hour, or minute, of his own bodily life can the Yogi exercise this power of transferring his *Atma,* or inner self, to the body of another?

"A. Until the last minute, or even second of his natural term of life. He knows beforehand to a second, when his body must die, and, until that second strikes, he may project his soul into another person's body if one is ready for his occupancy. But, should he allow that instant to pass, then he can do no more. The cord is snapped forever, and the Yogi, if not sufficiently purified and perfected to be enabled to obtain *Moksha,* must follow the common law of re-birth. The only difference between his case and that of other men is, that he, having become a far more intellectual, good and wise being than they, is re-born under better conditions.

"Q. Can a Yogi prolong his life to the following extent; say the natural life of his own body is seventy years, can he, just before the death of that body, enter the body of a child of six years, live in that another term of seventy years, remove from that to another, and live in it a third seventy?

"A. He can, and can thus prolong his stay on earth to about the term of four hundred years.

"Q. Can a Yogi thus pass from his own body into that of a woman?

"A. With as much ease as a man can, if he chooses, put on himself the dress of a woman, so he can put over his own *Atma* her physical form. Externally he would then be in every physical aspect and relation a woman; internally himself.

"Q. I have met two such; that is to say, two persons who appeared women, but who were entirely masculine in everything but the body. One of them, you remember, we visited together at Benares, in a temple on the bank of the Ganges,

"A. Yes, 'Majji.'

"Q. How many kinds of Yoga practice are there?

"A. Two—*Hatha Yoga and Raja Yoga.* Under the former the student undergoes physical trials and hardships for the purpose of subjecting his physical body to the will. For example, the swinging of one's body from a tree, head downwards, at a little distance from five burning fires, etc. In *Raja Yoga* nothing of the kind is required. It is a system of mental training by which the mind is made the servant of the will. The one—*Hatha Yoga*—gives physical results; the other—

Raja Yoga—spiritual powers. He who would become perfect in *Raja* must have passed through the training in *Hatha*.

"Q. But are there not persons who possess the *Siddhis,* or powers, of the *Raja Yoga,* without ever having passed through the terrible ordeal of the *Hatha?* I certainly have met three such in India, and they themselves told me they had never submitted their bodies to torture.

"A. Then they practiced *Hatha* in their previous birth."

Col. Olcott (whose entrance into India and Ceylon some twelve or more years ago, was owing to my having preceded him and later, further aiding him to the influential position that he now occupies in these countries, both as a Buddhist and a Hindu wearing the Sacred Cord), in an address previously delivered and published in the *Columbo Sandaresa,* April 6, 1906, the Colonel says: "While in America I happened to come across a pamphlet recording the proceedings of a discussion between the late Rev. Mr. Silva of the C. M. S., and Migettuwatte, the priest. I was very much struck with the force of the argument of the priest," etc.

While on my second journey around the world, nearly a generation ago, I stopped a month in Ceylon, studying the customs, manners, laws of the Sinhalese, and especially their religion, Buddhism. Hearing of this discussion at Pantura between a Christian preacher and the Buddhist, through considerable exertion at the printing offices I secured the reports (very imperfect) of the speeches made at this debate, and correcting, published them in a pamphlet (which I think of republishing) of a hundred pages, with annotations (an edition of 2,000). Owing to the native modesty and shrinking timidity (?) that afflicts many Americans, the Colonel in his address did not mention

In the *Colombo Buddhist,* of Sept. 2, 1892, occur
these words:

"The impressions of one's former life, or the
'accumulated experiences' are regarded as potent factors in the determination of one's re-birth. For instance, if a man persistently desires to eat animal food
like a tiger, and longs to have the appetite and strength
of that animal, it is possible that he may be born as a
tiger; but from that circumstance it should not be inferred that the nature of the tiger on this account will
improve."

A Hindu writer in the *Lahore (India) Harbinger,*
says:

"There are some people who have gone through the
human plane downward, that is, they have reached the
limit which is contiguous to the plane of the lower animals. As the influence of their wicked actions tends to
degrade them, they pass on to the sub-human plane,
which is occupied by the lower animals. They will then
appear in animal forms. . . . Our scriptures mention accounts of savages who passed into the bodies of
animals for a certain interval of time in expiation of
some sin."

---

my name as author of the pamphlet that by confession
took him to those oriental countries where he has
labored so effectually, especially in the interests of
theosophy, and Buddhism.

Personally, I have a very deep interest in Buddhism
—deep enough to purchase their literature, patronize
their press, lecture in its defense and twice contribut-
ing liberally financially to the support of Mrs. Higgin's
School for Buddhist Girls out at Cinnamon Gardens in
the suburbs of Colombo, verily a city of palms, blos-
soming vines and perpetual flowers.

In "Isis Unveiled," a rather lumbering book written after the formation of the Theosophical Society in New York, Col. Olcott wrote as follows:

"H. P. Blavatsky says most positively: 'We will now present a few fragments of this mysterious doctrine of reincarnation—as distinct from transmigration—which we have from an authority. Reincarnation, i. e., the appearance of the same individual, or rather of his astral monad, twice on the same planet, is not a rule in nature; it is an exception, like the teratological phenomenon of a two-headed infant.' The cause of it, when it does occur, is, she says that the design of nature to produce a perfect human being has been interfered with, and therefore she (Nature) must make another attempt. Such exceptional interferences, H. P. Blavatsky explains, are the cases of abortions, of infants dying before a certain age, and of congenital and incurable idiocy. If reason has been so far developed as to become active and discriminative, there is no reincarnation on this earth."

In commenting upon the above words of Madame Blavatsky, Colonel Olcott says in his *Theosophist,* Vol. III., No. 1:

"I believe that she wrote then (six years after the founding of the Theosophical Society) as she did later, exactly according to her lights, and that she was just as sincere in denying reincarnation in 1876-78 as she was in affirming it after 1882. Why she and I were permitted to put the misstatement into *Isis,* and, especially, why it was made to me by the Mahatma, I cannot explain, unless I was the victim of glamour in believing I talked with a master on the evening in question. So let it pass."

Apropos to the above, Alexander Fullerton, Secretary of the American Branch of Theosophists, wrote in the July *Theosophist*, 1902, as follows:

"H. P. Blavatsky must always remain the insoluble problem for Theosophists. Her marvelous powers, and her equally marvelous weaknesses, her inconsistences, her incompatibilities, the palpable facts which contradict the necessary facts—all make up a compound which can only be partially described or imperfectly grasped, and which cannot in the least be understood."

On the contrary, her "inconsistencies," her "marvelous weaknesses" and contradictions "can" be easily comprehended when it is understood as a fact that she was a spirit medium, not a spiritual, refined medium, but a spirit medium of the physical type, thinking, functioning on the astral earthly plane of consciousness. It was as unjust by high caste Brahmins as uncalled for to pronounce her without any qualifications a "black magician."

We are further informed by Mr. Fullerton (see *Theosophist*, July 2, 1902, Madras) that Madame Blavatsky first appeared as a "white magician." Mr. Fullerton, writing further in the *Theosophist* of a certain non-reconciliation, says:

"Col. Olcott has demonstrated that she knew nothing of reincarnation during her years in America, and that neither of them ever heard of it until they learned it in India; and yet it is *the vital doctrine* of the Theosophic philosophy, which she must have studied when in India before, also during her pupilship in Thibet. She was an advanced practical occultist when she first landed in the United States."

It was recently said in a noted monthly journal that it was not now taught that the spirits of mortals ever reincarnated into animals. This is not correct. This doctrine is taught and believed by the more or less uneducated in the Orient and by a few English-speaking people. To this end in *London Light,* December, 1901, occurs this statement:

"The medium being impelled to take a pencil, . . . wrote this under spirit control: 'I was a man on earth, but I was an unfaithful servant; I cheated and robbed and deceived my master, and now in the form of a dog, I am forced to learn what fidelity means.' "

Such statements I denominate the dark-eclipse side of the subject—a psychological exaggeration or a dreamy hallucination.

The late Dr. Helen Densmore, a most amiable and talented lady, of New York, in giving her reasons for re-embodiments, said: "That which coerced conviction of the correctness of reincarnation to my mind is the fact that it solves what had heretofore been insoluble problems, and makes consistent and simple what without this doctrine is chaos and night.

"I believe successive embodiments are a matter of choice after an adequate degree of evolution has been reached.

"I believe that the spirit enters upon embodiment at the moment of conception, and that the spirit builds the body and is not, as I formerly supposed, the result and product of the body.

"I believe that the soul is the source of consciousness in all human embodiments; that the spirit embodied is an expression of the soul, and that the soul is conscious not only while the spirit is 'secluding itself in another uterine imprisonment,' but is also conscious of all preceding embodiments. I will refer to this matter further on.

"A mother can tell to a certainty by her own state of development of the general scope and nature of the one about to be embodied. Like attracts like. A New Zealand cannibal mother is not able to attract a saint, and is in no danger of giving embodiment to one; and a mother with a saintly nature and aspiration is in no danger of giving birth to a New Zealand cannibal.

"Philosophy has always taught the all-wise justice and beneficence of the Supreme Power, and yet it is perfectly plain to an unprejudiced mind that there can be no justice in the creation of one human being who suffers a series of calamities through life and dies an outcast, while there is created another human being whose life runs smoothly and is filled with happiness and content, providing these two lives end the matter.

"The question is asked at once and always, why this difference? and there is no other system of philosophy that reconciles this inequality and injustice. The system of successive embodiments explains perfectly that, while one individual has the most fortunate conditions and circumstances in one life, in another he has had or will have as great misfortunes as any; and, moreover, those that are seen in this life to be suffering from untoward misfortunes are sure in some other embodiment to achieve blessings equal to the greatest. Absolute justice requires absolute democracy. There must be equality of conditions and destinies or else there is injustice. But there is no way possible for anyone else to explain away the manifest injustices of this life on any other hypothesis than that of successive embodiments." *

---

* See "A discussion on reincarnation between Dr. Densmore and Dr. Peebles"—both sides—106 page pamphlet, neatly bound. Battle Creek, Michigan. Price 40 cents, postage 5 cents.

In a multitude of counselors it is said there is wisdom. Justice demands a fair, unprejudiced presentation of the best and of all sides to a moral equation. The learned Mortimer Stuart, dissenting from Dr. Densmore, gives rational reasons for reincarnation from both the Hindu and Buddhist view-point. Here follow his words:

"Human reincarnation, according to Hindu thought is a cyclic necessity not to be dreaded, though the necessity for it may be deplored. But Buddha taught a way of avoiding this necessity in his doctrine of poverty, restriction of the senses, perfect indifference to the objects of earthly desire, freedom from passion, and frequent intercommunication with the Atma— that is to say, soul-contemplation. The cause of reincarnation, in this view, is ignorance of our senses and the idea that there is any reality in the world, anything except abstract existence—pure spirit."

"It is not the false personality, the illusive human entity defined and individualized during this brief temporal life under some specific form and name, that is reincarnated. What must reincarnate, according to Karmic law, is the real Ego, and a confusion between the immortal Ego in man and the changing, temporary personalities it inhabits, lies at the root of many misunderstandings as to the real nature of the doctrine."

Dr. Paul Carus, author of "The Soul of Man," "Chinese Philosophy," "Buddhism," etc., assures us in these words that:

"Our life does not begin with birth nor does it conclude with death. It is only a section of the development of mankind before and after us. We existed before we were born and we reap what the factors of our being have sown. So our life leaves its after effects and they will be what we have made them.''

Let us turn over a new leaf and read from a brighter chapter of poesy and philosophy. Under all dogmas, however distorted, there are gems and pearls of truth. The wise find them. Both póets and philosophers are inspired from the spiritual heavens.

"Not from the blank Inane emerged the soul:
A sacred treasury it is of dreams
And deeds that built the present from the past,
Adding thereto its own experiences.
Ancestral lives are seeing in mine eyes,
Their hearing listeneth within my ears,
And in my hand their strength is plied again.
Speech came, a rich consignment from the past,
Each word aglow with wondrous spirit life,
Thus building up my soul of myriad souls.''

CHAPTER XI.

"Where are the swelling majesties of old,
The kings who built on skulls and emptiness?
Where Ninus, with the dove upon his shield?
His name is now a whisper from the dust
That once was Nineveh, that once was pride.

"And where is Rameses, the king of kings?
He has gone down to nothingness and night.
One sunken stone beside the dateless Nile
Stammers to Time his ineffectual fame.

. . . .

"Love stays—it can change bare rafters to a home
Sweetened with hopes and hushed with memories;
Can change a pit into a holy tomb
Where pilgrims keep the watches of the night;
Can change an earthly face until it shine,
Touched with unearthly beauty. In its might
A reed did at once become a scepter—yea,
A cross became a throne; a crown of thorns
A symbol of the Power above the world."

Among the sound thinkers and scholarly writers of
the latter part of the last and the beginning of this
twentieth century, is Prof. E. Whipple, of San Diego,
California. For years he was a lecturer upon the
natural sciences, moral philosophy and various psychic
phenomena. He is still in the harvest field of study,
but sounds no trumpet, seeks no exaltation, nor did he
ever strive to reach the summit of fame by rudely

trampling upon others, who in different directions were
seeking the priceless pearl of truth. In the following
pages he presents the philosophy of reincarnation in
its most attractive and convincing manner. It is to be
regretted that there could not have been in the past
more agreement upon the insoluble principles and
methods of the spirit's "career."

"O mortal, who art immortal;
  Thou who in clay partaketh of the Eternal;
  Canst thy soul pierce the Darkness?
  Canst thou read the Hidden?"

What I shall now attempt to embody, writes the professor, is, in part, a logical deduction from the postu-
late of man's pre-existence; in part, also, the purport
of communications made to me at different times, and
in different countries, by a purporting high order of
spirits. Their testimonies are to me more suggestive
than authoritative. And I will add, that what I am
about to state, is not offered as a strict result of science,
nor is it offered dogmatically as something which you
must believe. It is merely an abstract of my own cosmical conception of the way in which the matter lies
in my mind at present, as a result of all that I know,
combined with things which I have been told and
largely believed. It is a sort of conclusions which may
need much revision when I become older, wiser and
more ripened in a knowledge of divine things. It claims
no authority other than such as may come from its own
intrinsic reasonableness. In the interests of brevity,
and to avoid tedious metaphysical distinctions I have
used the words ego, soul, spirit synonymously.

PRELIMINARY REFLECTIONS.

The belief that the conscious spirit traverses a succession of careers on the material plane has been almost universal in history, both among oriental and occidental civilizations, notably among the most learned of the ancient Egyptians, Chaldeans, Hindus and Greeks; and in the West it has been diffused through the Toltec, Aztec and Inca nations, including their priests and sovereigns. Nor will it be disputed that this philosophy is to-day rapidly spreading among all the English speaking populations. Many causes conspire to this result. Civilization has reached a bead in the road where many new aspects come into view—psychic, religious and social. Here men of different beliefs and with different traditions accost each other and compare notes. The Orient pours its rich intellectual treasures into the Occident. Long buried cities are being disentombed. The archeological and philological treasures from long perished empires have been made accessible to us. The sea of ancient wisdom is giving up its dead. Scholars evince an interest in these themes beyond what has ever before been experienced, and gradually this interest extends to the outer surface of society and takes hold on the common people. Lytton writes his marvelous stories of ''Zanoni'' and the ''Coming Race,'' half fact, half fiction, and now books are rapidly multiplying to satisfy the popular hunger for truths of the inner light and life. Indeed, the public mind is unconsciously preparing for the advent of a new condition and a new departure in modes of thinking and acting.

"In the Paradise-sphere of God there's a Fountain
Embowered around by olive trees and palms,
The sun ariseth in its bosom,
The golden stars emerge from its silver zone,
Blue are its shining waters,
Of a deep blue like a child's dark eyes.
And when its ripples glitter in the sunlight,
They are as a thousand flashing emeralds.
O pilgrim of God! seeketh thou this Fountain?
Wouldst thou taste its sweet waters?
O wanderer of Eternity, follow
And I will lead thee to its green solitude."

I conceive the universe to be distributed upon three
fundamental planes corresponding to the factors of
substance, force and form.

1. Upon the material plane substance is precipitated in the chemical units so familiar to the physicist.
And the various combinations resulting from their
union constitute our physical world—our material environment.

2. Upon the spiritual plane, corresponding to the
active principle or force, it is not only conceivable, but
reasonable, that substance is precipitated in forms
quite unlike the chemical units with which we are
familiar. These again aggregate in an environment
appropriate to this higher octave in the scale of nature.

3. The celestial embraces still another octave, with
scenes, circumstances and higher agencies to corre-
spond.

Upon the lower plane, matter and passivity are re-
latively predominant. Upon the second or spiritual
plane the positive and projective forces are predominant. The celestial unites the two polar spheres in a
higher unity. I conceive, therefore, that the totality
of movement necessitates an interchange of forms and

forces between these three fundamental states of being.

The celestial realm, so nearly allied to absolute spirit, is largely the sphere of causes. Some spirits denominate it the sun sphere. Earth-bound spirits for long periods, have little or no conception of it. The conscious spirit is the essential man, and man's original home was in the celestial heavens. On earth he is a voluntary sojourner. Some spirits, however, as the Rev. Charles Beecher teaches, may be exiles. Be this as it may, all spirits by methods inverse and diverse, tend homeward. The time may be long, the way thorny! David had not returned in the apostles' time to his celestial home. These are the apostolic words,—"For David is not ascended into the heavens."

"To God again the enfranchised soul must tend,
He is her home, her Author is her end;
No death is hers; when earthly eyes grow dim
Starlike she soars and Godlike melts in Him."

Experience is the choicest of school-masters; and experiences imply activities—and active labors necessitate repose. Accordingly something as the body requires periodical repose to replenish the energies expended in the walking hours, so the perpetuity of the conditions essential to the super-sensual activity in the celestial state involves not only a sort of spiritual repose, but an interchange with the negative—the material pole of nature. As the material world is dependent upon the celestial for the types and germinal forms necessary to imitate organic processes and material development, so the celestial is dependent upon those forms of force that act from a material base to maintain the balance of movement in its own higher domains. So in like manner we may rationally persuade ourselves

8

that exalted personalities in the celestial world, recognizing the conditions essential to universal harmony,
volunteer to spend a fraction of their time in this material world of existence. We honor the kind-hearted
English professor who volunteered to leave his college
class and teach a term in a ragged school of London.
Our world is peopled with exiles from choice and exiles
from necessity—each and all were pre-existent.

Few believe that God, by a special act, manufac-
tures the immortal spirit at either conception or birth.
And a still less number will hazard the opinion that the
thinking, reasoning spirit was evolved from unthink-
ing, unreasoning matter. If this latter theory be true,
then it is certain that effects may exceed their causes—
that streams may arise above their fountains. Neither
matter nor blind force, singly nor in conjunction, can
generate conscious life. Water neither thinks nor
feels when it runs down into frost-ferns upon a window-
pane. Earthquakes do not reason. Gravity does not
think; nor do gravity and a rock bounding, dashing
down a mountain-side create butterflies and birds;
nor can two human beings constituted of matter and
force, create or bring into the world through birth, a
conscious immortal being. Such a theory is its own
refutation.

Modern writers of materialistic tendencies who talk
and write incessantly of evolution, write and talk of
only one-half of the uses and methods connected with
the universe. They fail to recognize the law of re-
ciprocity—the balance of forces. They do not see that
evolution implies involution. The one necessitates the
other. A philosophy predicated upon evolution alone
is comparable to a boatman struggling to cross a lake
with only one oar. His wriggling, zig-zag motions,

exciting pity, prophesy of disaster. It is, therefore, important to remember that "involution" is the process of storing up, folding away, holding the forces or faculties in tension, and of transferring hidden energy into active energy.

Evolution is the process by which the potential is liberated, made active, unfolded and brought forth into the actual, or what some would denominate outward expression.

Now, then, when the divine soul-germ, when essential inmost man becomes incarnate in the sacred moment of embryotic conception, he may be said to have entered the state of involution; and he continues largely in that state during his imprisonment in, or direct connection with the material body. And further, it may be stated that while in this state of involution, disordered by passion, and beclouded by sense or sense perceptions, the cases are rare where man's powers of reminiscence are sufficiently potent to project themselves into the outer realms of memory and external consciousness. But the failure to remember is no proof against pre-existence. The events of our infancy are not remembered. In early childhood we smiled, wept, and played with the rattle, but no traces of them ripple upon the sea of external memory in the present. Infantile existence is as difficult of memory as pre-existence.

"Light of the Universe!
When shall I return to thee?
When shall I go back unto the ancient places,
The paradise bowers of Primeval Love?
My spirit longs for its antecedent home.
.   .   .   .

O ye waves and water of beauty,
Gleaming like the white-footed of heaven.

.   .   .   .

Afar off did I behold the King of Spirits,
Whose head was like the snows.''

MY OWN COSMICAL CONCEPTION.

I consider this world a sort of hotel for spiritual
beings on pilgrimages, a sort of school for culture and
discipline, a realm for observation and the treasuring
of experiences. This universe is made up of the aggregate of the Cosmical Conceptions which are entertained
by all of us; that is to say, by all beings capable of
having mental conceptions. Some one exclaimed:
''What a different universe for Newton, and Newton's
dog Carlo!'' To be sure! And what a different universe for any two of us! It is not sufficiently reflected
upon that we all inhabit different worlds, or world-
ideas. It is this which I mean by Cosmical Conception,
and in that aspect of it especially which relates to the
spirit's pilgrimage in matter.

I conceive, then, of this universe as of a three-
storied edifice, of which this outer and lower, or mundane world, may be taken as the lower, or foundation story, and the entire spirit world, as that term is
ordinarily understood, as a second and intermediate
story; or, if you will, one more interior and retired,
as we have, in entering the second story, to go in and
up through that which is below. There is, then, a third
story, a sort of dome or observatory, more interior, and
higher still, which overlooks the whole edifice, and, as
it were, dominates the whole. Let us denominate this the
Eternal Spiritual World, or the loftier realm of the

Highest and Inmost. The entire etheric-world, as such, including the three Heavens and the three Hells of Swedenborg and his intermediate world of Spirits, and including the prevalent Seven-sphere doctrine of the early Modern Spiritualists, is, then, an intermediate world between this outer mundane world, and the Inmost, the Eternal Spiritual-World, or the Olympian Heights of the Cosmos.

I believe that individual human spirits are directly born through the spirit world, out of the Eternal Spiritual-World, into this outer mundane world; and when the body assumed here dies, the spirit falls back into the spirit world; and subsequently, by another process it recedes again, no matter after how many centuries, into the inmost; or, otherwise conceived, arises to the utmost subjective heights of its own divine nature. At this sublime and centering point of being I conceive that all spirits who arrive there—or rather when they arrive there, as all do at recurring periods of their external existence—are freed to the greatest possible degree, but never absolutely, from their connection with subtile matter; and that they are, at this point, absorbed into the Divine Sphere, or, in simple terms, into God. Here spirits form a complex unity—a unity, nevertheless, which is never so absolute as to imply loss of individuality, for the real spirit never occupies any station where self-consciousness is more acute and luminous.

It is this close verging of unity upon nothingness which was felt or perceived by the old Hindoo philosophers, whence arose the fact that absorption into God was by them confounded with annihilation, and called Nirvana, a word which has that meaning. But passages constantly occur in the theological writings of that wonderful period of thought and philosophy which are inconsistent with the idea of nothingness, and which restore the notion of unity. Nirvana, the Divine Sphere, the Supreme God-realm, was, in fact, to their conception, the wavering margin between annihilation and the absolute fulness of being, the conceptual cleft between Aught and Naught, out of which all things proceed, the point to which Hegel again brings back the beginning of philosophy.

"When traveling in Buddhistic Ceylon, in the year 1878, I sought," wrote Dr. Peebles, "an audience with the Ceylonese Arch-Priest H. Sumangala, that I might interrogate him regarding the Buddhist's doctrine of Nirvana. Our U. S. Consul and his interpreter accompanied me out to the Buddhist College in Colombo, the grounds of which were beautified with palms and oriental shrubbery. There I had a long talk with the arch-priest upon Nirvana and other subjects. He said the Northern and Southern Buddhists differed about Nirvana something as Christians do about the real meaning of Heaven. He further said: 'Nirvana to me means the complete and total extinction of individual consciousness—absorption into the universal ocean of Spirit. When you leave this temple,' he continued, 'what will you carry away with you?' I replied, I will carry away my memory of it. He added: 'But memory fails! Where are your baby hairs? They have returned to the great vortex of matter. You forget your baby cries, your childhood thoughts. They are forever gone! As you become more refined, more etherial, more spiritualized, you will at last like the drop of water become absorbed in the infinite ocean of Spirit.' I was silent. But I reflected that the priest's conclusions were perfectly logical from his pantheistic or materialistic premises."

In the far East the doctrine of reincarnation as taught by the oriental adepts has degenerated into strange notions of metapsychosis and transmigration. All the Buddhist priests with whom I conversed in Ceylon and the Brahmin priests in India held some form of the general theory of reincarnation degenerated into transmigration. They believe the man who lives a good and upright life, will, in the next career, incarnate in a human form and will be better conditioned than in the previous career. But if the man live a life of low cunning and intrigue, he will next incarnate in a fox or jackal. If his life was habitually cruel, he will next incarnate in a tiger, and so on. Man, attaching himself to evil, falls at death into such an animal state as corresponds with the turpitude of his soul, which may be so great as to cast him down again into the lowest point of existence, whence he shall again return through such a succession of animal existences as are most proper to divest him of his evil propensities.

Here it may be proper to parenthetically insert the Buddhist sevenfold classification of man. This classification embraces a Lower Quarternary and an Upper Traid: First—Rupa, the *Sthula Sarira* or physical body; second—the *Prana, Jiva* or life-essence; third—the Astral Body, double or image of the man; fourth —*Kama Rupa* or animal soul; fifth—*Manas*, the higher intelligence, the persistent ego that incarnates in a succession of forms; sixth—*Buddhi*, the Spiritual soul or inmost vehicle of the ego; seventh—*Atma*, the Source and Fountain which is pure Spirit.

Buddhism assumes that at death—or soon after— the Lower Quarternary is dissipated; that the Upper Triad, through the Manas or Fifth Principle, rein-

carnates in a succession of human forms; but that
finally the last vehicle will be dissolved by the disap-
pearance of the Fifth and Sixth Principles, when Atma
will become restored to the undifferentiated ocean of
pure Spirit. But to resume.

In the true identification of the Spirit with Supreme
Being, the individual spirit becomes divine, or rather
resumes that divinity which is always inherent in it,
constituting the inmost of every being.

At this sublime elevation the immortal spirit looks
out with a free vision over the universal realm. It
runs back on the lines of its own past careers into the
infinity of the past, and forward over other careers
which lie prospectively before it. It is endowed with
a qualified omnipotence and omniscience—an omnipotence and omniscience only limited by laws which are
cognate with its own nature, and by the coincidence of
other individualities with which, as involved in the
same divine sphere, it finds itself in perfect harmony.

The individual Spirit, lodged in this divine sphere,
in this eternal spiritual-world, dwell there—as I conceive—at its own option, through countless ages; or,
from motives which affect it, it determines in freedom,
and from its own choice, to enter upon some new career
through the lower realms of less purified spirit, and
of gross matter. In this latter case it selects and plans
its voyage, even down to a certain degree of the
minutiæ of detail. It puts itself under the guardian-
ship of such as remain, and launches out upon its new
and perilous voyage. It selects the parentage of its
own future body, watches over its evolution, enters
it as a new born being at the appropriate moment, purposely cuts off its memory of its own high estate, and
so renews the journey of life in the lower spheres, not

as a culprit condemned to serve out a penitential destiny, but in full freedom and from its own individual choice.

As before remarked, the conscious spirit at its own sublime height is intact, independent, and has the voluntary power to go out from its subjective state of being and project itself into form. The inmost or supreme in man is supreme over circumstance. Let me illustrate by analogies: Suppose a prince, born at a court, and destined to the inheritance of royalty. There is no external and constraining necessity compelling him to undergo hardship or to accept of a career of severity and endurance. But he has heard of sailors and voyages and shipwrecks, and of wars and warriors and battles, and his very spirit becomes fired with the love of adventure or with stern ambition of hardihood, and he determines to test the troubles of that lower order of life which he is alike free to avoid. But he does not wish to cut himself off absolutely from the advantages of his high station, so he selects some friend at court and charges him with the duty of overlooking his necessities, providing funds and acquaintanceship, and other reliefs at the various ports at which he may touch, and he takes his departure under this contingent protection. This oversight illustrates the whole doctrine of guardian angels.

The prince provides or selects his particular ship, as the spirit does its particular child-body, and shuts himself in like another Moses in his boat of bulrushes, for the voyage of life, with all its hardships and adventure. To make the experiment perfect, he should, as he does, cut off absolutely or nearly so, his memory of his own exalted native condition, and identify himself to the utmost with the new order of life. He is not

content to enter by the cabin windows. He doesn't
want a sham exposure, but a real exposure to the trials
of the mundane sphere. He must not, therefore, have
too much recollection and consciousness. So he enters
before the mast. He becomes a common sailor; he
undergoes every test, performs every duty, or he fails
to do so and suffers the penalty. Perhaps he rises
through the ranks, and comes out an admiral. This
may be likened to the death which removes the individual from earth into the spirit-world, on his way back
to the eternal spirit-world. And finally, at option, he
resumes his original high estate, or returns home
strengthened and enriched by manifold experiences.

Or suppose, instead, an actress, not driven by stress
of circumstances, but by the inward suggestions of her
own genius to select the histrionic career. As she goes
from the green-room before the foot-lights, she dis-
robes herself as absolutely as possible of her own self-
hood—cuts off her memory of who and what she is—
and identifies herself with the role she is about to
enact. When she returns to the green-room, she dis-
robes herself again of her role and resumes her self-
hood.

The three lives which have been sketched are never,
however, wholly distinct. They interpenetrate each
other, and it may chance, by contract of extremes, that
some in the lower or mundane sphere are in closer communion with the supreme life than any in the intermediate life. As there is a strong sympathy between
the old and the young, between the Czar and the common people, between the highest and the lowest, this
kind of rapport is to be anticipated. But we enter
here upon a new and immense series of speculations,
for which time does not now serve.

CHAPTER XII.

———

"Oh, yes we trust somehow good
   Shall be the final end of ill,
   To pangs of nature, sins of will,
Defects of doubt, and taints of blood.

That nothing walks with aimless feet;
   That not one life shall be destroyed
   Or cast as rubbish on the void
When God hath made the pile complete."

QUALIFYING STATEMENTS.

At this point it may be proper to make a provisional qualification to what has been given above, touching the freedom of the spirit in choosing its own material theater. It is more than probable that the spirits above alluded to constitute an exceptional class, the members of which long since graduated from the school of material struggle and experience, having traversed their necessary rounds through a long succession of careers. Emerging from their probationary stat they are now free to descend, choose their parentage, assume fleshy garments and labor to instruct and lift up the earth lives. To this class belong such great spirits as Buddha, Jesus, Mohammed and others. These regal spirits are not bound within the evolutionary processes now manifest on earth, but voluntarily co-operate and work with them. As I said, these exalted spirits are voluntary laborers on the earth and in the heavens of the earth, giving special direction to the movements of nations at the turning points of crisis periods in their history. In this manner Jesus gave a special direction to the evolutionary phases of the Western nations by dating the Christian Dispensation.

Now, as we view the present population of our globe, we must regard its major portion as not yet included among that hierarchy of angelic spirits, the members of which long since graduated out of the lesson schools of earth and other planets. The spirit in its first estate may be regarded as supreme on its own plane—in its own subjective domain. But to be able to traverse all planes and interchange at will between the subjective and objective poles of universal nature,—this involves successive rounds of experience on all the planes below. And for this experience the spirit must fashion for itself a suitable mechanism as a vehicle for expression. In the final round a Body-Form must be achieved which shall stand as the complete embodiment and complement of the full-orbed spirit. This will be a universal body. It will be an immortal body. It will be the body which the traditional resurrection faintly typifies. It will be a body in which the spirit will be free to express its transcendant powers on every plane of existence, from the innermost to the outermost. I know this is directly opposed to the pantheistic and theosophic view—that we must get rid of organism instead of achieving it. But here opens a large field and I must defer its discussion to some future period.

On its first entrance into matter the spirit inherits

difficulty. It must gain a knowledge of material laws and phenomena through experience. It must climb the ladder of attainment through slow and difficult ascents. To make material knowledge thorough and exhaustive, the spirit must take lessons in a vast number of primary schools. It must be permitted to behold the panorama of nature through the eyes of many nations, races and ages. It must experience all imaginable incentives to action and encounter all possible resistances to its attainment. Poverty and hardship must oft be its portion. Affluence, power and splendor may at long recurring intervals be enjoyed. The spirit's ultimate goal is material conquest and mental freedom, and the careers will be multiplied until this conquest and freedom are achieved.

As I conceive, this larger class who are still held within the limitations of the evolutionary law are constrained within comparatively narrow bounds. Having entered into the evolutionary process of this planet, they must abide by the law of those processes until their evolution is completed. The individual has no choice as to whether he shall incarnate once or a thousand times. than a soldier when received into the army has of electing his own independent course of action. The spirit was originally free to descend for the purpose of acquiring experience as the recruit was of enlisting, but having once committed itself to the earth careers, it must share the incidents of the long and perilous journey. When the natural law prescribes the Ego's return into a fleshy tabernacle, he must abide by its decree. Nor do I suppose that at the threshold of a new birth he is in any sense conscious of what lies before him, for the record of the previous life is sealed up and held potential against the day when all the records of all the careers will be unsealed in the body of the "Resurrection." Each career constitutes a separate chapter in the life-volume the spirit is writing, and this chapter must be wrought out on its own particular merits.

OPINIONS ON REINCARNATION—DOGMATIC, AXIOMATIC AND OTHERWISE.

The author of "The Light of Egypt" dogmatically asserts: "Once and only once is the law. After this nature shuts the door. . . . Those who hold the strangely illogical doctrine of a multiplicity of births, have certainly never evolved the lucid state of spirit-consciousness in themselves." And yet this self-assertive writer who "knows whereof he affirms," admits the following exceptions to the law of "once and only once." First—"cases of abortion or of still-born children . . . generally become reincarnated. Second—cases of natural born idiots. Though it is very rare that even idiots are so lost to all external consciousness as to make re-birth necessary to them. Third—cases of special Messianic incarnation by exalted spirits for the special purpose of enlightening the race." The laws which govern this latter mystery are known only to the author of "The Light of Egypt" and the "highest adepts(?)" I should like to ask if the idiot is permitted to come again, where is the law of justice which denies a second or third trial to one just above the idiot?

This author admits a pre-existent monad and its incarnation in a multitude of forms, but asserts that all these incarnations occur below the plane of the human. He holds that this monad descends to the lowest point of mineral life through a long series of involutions through every state of the soul-world, the Astral Kingdom, and so on until it reaches the lowest mineral state on the terrestrial plane. From this point the monad ascends by evolution through the three Kingdoms in nature until it reaches the summit of the animal. Having reached the human plane the privileges become abridged, and the law declares, "only once." This may be fairly considered among the hypotheses current at the present day; but its dogmatic assertion is by no means a good recommendation for its general acceptance.

The modern Christian theory, which supposes the creation of a new spirit at each birth, has become nearly obsolete. If the theological dogma which asserts that the child who dies at birth is surely saved, the Christian who really believes it ought to return devout thanks when the grave closes over the forms of their little ones. This theory, together with a modification of it held by many Spiritualists, postulates an immortal existence with only one end to it. To the rational mind this is as absurd as it is illogical.

I think no one will deny that material knowledge can best be acquired through a physical body—by an organism in immediate contact with a material environment. And I submit that one brief career, wrought out under almost every imaginable disadvantage, within the circumscribed area of an island in mid-ocean or a remote mountain hamlet, with a diseased and imperfect inheritance, is not only lamentably inadequate for the proper functioning of the spirit, but it affords such a paucity of experience of the laws of phenomena of the objective domain, as to raise the question of flagrant injustice somewhere by this cutting the aspirational spirit off from all further opportunity for acquiring both knowledge and perfection of the organic mechanism, in this most essential department of the universe.

I am persuaded that the most of us but half appreciate the value of knowledge and experience derived on the material plane of existence. I believe this knowledge should be as complete, exhaustive and universal as the entire domain of physical nature. Not only this, but the human spirit having once entered into a physical world, should not be compelled to quit it until it has achieved an objective organism which shall be the exact complement and counterpart of the Ego on its own subjective plane. Such an ultimate organism may be properly regarded as the end and purpose for which the spirit connected itself with material existence. This would be the crown and fulfillment of all the earth careers. And this sublime culmination would be ample compensation for all the struggles and sorrow incident to this long and toilsome journey. The spirit's pilgrimage in matter is the outworking of a wise design, not an expiation as a consequence of a fatal curiosity to taste the sweets of sensuous experience.

The Body of the "Resurrection" is the Great Fulfillment, for then—and not until then will the human Ego be fully equipped for its proper place and function in the universe,—a resurrection, not of this old, diseased, rickety, imperfect and worn out physical body, but a resurrection of the essential acquisitions and memories of all the antecedent careers. These, brought to one focus and centered in one immortal structure, will stand as the full blossom and fruit of the spirit's fashioning under the laws of material evolu-

tion. This will be the attained summit, enduring mon-
ument of all the special lives—*the glorified Body* such
as Jesus demonstrated to his disciples before his
Ascension.''

" 'Tis told somewhere in Eastern story
    That those who loved once blossomed as flowers
On the same stem, amid the glory
    Of Eden's green and fragrant bowers,
And that, though parted oft by Fate,
    Yet when the glow of life is ended,
Each soul again shall find its mate,
    And in one bloom again be blended.''

9

CHAPTER XIII.

"If yon bright stars which gem the night
    Be each a blissful dwelling sphere,
Where *kindred spirits* re-unite,
    Whom death hath torn asunder here.

"How sweet it were at once to die,
    And leave this blighted orb, afar
Mixt soul with soul, to cleave the sky,
    And soar away from star to star.

"But Oh! how dark, how drear and lone
    Would seem the brightest world of bliss,
If, wandering through each *radiant zone*,
    We failed to find the loved of this."

                          —*Wm. Leggett.*

Now—you have read and considered the testimonies in the past pages of this book relating to pre-existence and reincarnation, the latter having been presented from its lowest and highest aspects—and you—you are the jurors. Consider first then, these words of Dr. Gregory, Edinburg, Scotland:

"The most cautious philosopher has no right to reject well-attested facts because he cannot see or comprehend their explanation, and certainly he has no right to charge witnesses with deed or imposture before he has himself fully and carefully inquired into them. If he will not, he cannot, inquire, it is only proper that he should be silent; to do otherwise is as unjust as it is irrational.''

To get at the root of these momentous matters, let us begin as near as possible to the root-principle— God. Definitions of God are as useless as impossible, because the inferior can neither comprehend nor define the superior. But thoughtful opinions and conceptions are ever admissible upon this subject, so prominent, so studied through all the agone ages; therefore the following:

"God is Causation.''—*Proclus.*

"God is Spirit.''—*Jesus.*

"God is the great Positive Mind.—*A. J. Davis.*

"God is the Supreme Mind of the universe.''
                                        —*A. R. Wallace.*

"God is Love.''—*Apostle John.*

"God is our loving Father.''—*Channing.*

"God is our Father-Mother.''—*Ann Lee.*

"God is the Infinite and Eternal Energy from which all things proceed.''—*Spencer.*

"God is that power, *not ourselves,* which makes for righteousness.''—*Arnold.*

"God is Absolute Being, manifest throughout all nature as energy, life and consciousness, as love, purpose and will.''—*Peebles.*

"God, The Supreme Being—the most essential element in Christianity, is not God apart from the universe, but immanent and actually incarnate in it, as life and will.''—*Sir Oliver Lodge.*

"God, the immanent, the intramundane and transcendent life of all things that were and are.''
                                        —*Sankhya.*

The conceptions of Proclus and Jesus relating to

the Divine Presence are taken as the foundation of
our reasoning because they are the most concise.

While there is everywhere manifest an Infinite and
Eternal Energy—God—there is something *that is not
God*. For the want of a better descriptive word we
will call it *substance,* the negative side of Being. This
inconceivable realm of substance, nebula, monads,
atoms, fire-dust and infinitesimal entities, when manipulated and moved upon become matter, a temporary
appearance cognized by the sense-perceptions; we say
temporary, because granite itself submitted to a very
intense degree of heat melts, becomes a liquid, a gas,
and vanishes into the invisible. Every appearance
must have a corresponding base—a reality. None will
contend that the thing moved moves itself—that the
thing developed develops itself, or that the thing
evolved evolves itself, independent of some causative,
propelling power. Life springing into conscious existence from non-life is as unthinkable as the deriva-
tion of something from nothing. Neither man nor his
ennobling religious emotions originated from the
chance-force friction of atoms nor from any blind
polarized interblendings of unreasoning molecules.
These of themselves could never produce such desir-
able fruitage as morality and religion—that religion
pure and undefiled which makes for righteousness and
heaven here and now, and for beatific blessedness hereafter.

And so reasoning from the known to the unknown,
we see God as causation incarnated—embodied in the
measureless universe, and every sun a mighty ganglion
and every galaxy of stars a nervous plexus, and every
tree and plant and flower a vital corpuscle in the cosmos; while through this infinitude of worlds and forces,

the positive acting upon the plastic, are diffused inter-blending chords and currents and series of movements implying interchanging actions, rounds of reincarnations and pulsating harmonies.

The divine incarnation in human flesh, idealized in the sacred symbols of the Babylonian, Hebraic, Platonian dispensations—was idealized in other and all the cycles of human history—idealized in ancient architectural temples which were representative of that truer and higher temple in which the spirit of God dwells; the human body thus practically exemplifying the prophetically inspired truth of the regenerative Logos—"the word made flesh and dwelling among men"—Emanuel, God with us and God in us, looking forward to that perfected man on this planet who can say—"I and my Father are one."

That dispensations come and go like sea-waves—that there is a law of cycles in history corresponding to the continuity of life, none who have studied this subject deny. And why should the human spirit be an exception to this law?

What is the spirit?

This inquiry has been briefly answered in a previous chapter; and yet we may further say that the adepts of the Orient call the spirit—the divine inmost, *the Atma*—the higher self—the center of moral gravitation in man—the incarnate God in activity—a conscious spark from the Infinite fire and life of the universe. This indivisible, uncompounded unit of consciousness is the bed-rock anchor of immortality. It is not a make-up from animals, nor from or by animal-excited mortals in generation, neither is it an aggregate of elements and atoms, which some superior, potent force may disintegrate, scattering the aggregated particles, and destroying consciousness—the moral equivalent of annihilation—pantheistic atheism.

What are we to understand by consciousness?

Tyndal, agnostic yet liberal, writing of cosmic law and matter, saw in it the "potency and promise of terrestrial life;" while Sir William Crookes, an abler scientist and psychist, says without any modification: "I should prefer to reverse the apothegm and to say that in life I see the promise and potency of all forms of matter."

Treating upon this same subject, the permanency of life and consciousness, Fiske in his "Darwinianism" writes—"Nowhere is there such a thing as the metamorphosis of motion into feeling or of feeling into motion. Instead of entering into the dynamic circuit of correlated physical motions, the phenomena of consciousness stand outside as utterly alien and disparate phenomena." And if Descartes had formulated his famous proposition, *cogito ergo sum* (I think, therefore, I am) in these words: "I consciously feel, therefore I am," his statement would have been beyond the touch of the most ingenious sophist.

The erudite Professor Hopkins said: "Whatever consciousness may be, there are three characteristics attributed to it by common consent, and these it must have. The first is, as its etymology, con-scio, implies, that it can never be alone. It must always accompany some other operation of the mind, and does in fact equally accompany all mental operations. The second characteristic is that it must be infallible, must be something that never does, or can, deceive us. The third characteristic is that consciousness is not a separate faculty, but is involuntary; is alike in all the race; and is a necessary act concomitant with all mental acts of which we know anything. It has an equal and common relation to all the faculties and is correlated to the inmost spirit.''

This illustrious thinker further defines consciousness as "the knowledge by the mind of itself as the permanent and indivisible subject of its own operations. This implies a knowledge of the operations, but leaves that knowledge to be given by its own specific faculty while consciousness holds the whole in unity by a constant reference of the different acts and states of the mind to the indivisible self or ego." And lying at the root of all knowledge is an inner, interior illumination, all of which may be summed up thus: I a spirit, know that I know, and while difficult to project what I know through these fleshly vestures, I know that it is the same I that knows, and the same I that is conscious of my consciousness, and the same I that feels, purposes and wills.

And this I, a potentialized and infinitesimal portion of the Conscious Life of the universe, reigns supreme over and illumines the human form. The lights in a candelabrum in the room, though related to and lighting the room, are neither the room itself nor the furniture in the room. And so this indivisible, indissoluble spirit, the real self, related to God and the crowned King of the human body, guides the corpuscles, atoms, molecules, cells, nerves—all these, they being his subjects.

And if wise enough, potent enough and sufficiently familiar with the psychic auras and the magnetic forces connected with the physical, mental and spiritual make-up of the human body, the spirit can leave it and return to it. This occurs in the higher class of dreams, and also in trance-conditioned states aided by discarnate intelligences. This conscious spirit may also for purposes planned in the heavens, dwell for a time in another bodily organization.

The well-conceived work, "Dr. Jekyll and Mr. Hyde," by Robert Louis Stevenson, whose tomb I visited upon reaching Samoa on a journey around the world, though seemingly a parable is really the philosophy of a series of facts—a brilliant gem set in beautiful imagery. It implies the possibility, and indirectly the method by which a positive personality may first psychically hypnotize, then control, and finally possess the person, the possessed being as unlike his real, conscious self as sunshine is unlike shadow.

Psychic obsession and possession logically account for the underlying facts, hazy, ambiguously-worded sentences appearing in psychic research reports and various magazines—"dual personalities," "subconscious personalities," "triune personalities," "duplex lives," and kindred mystic verbiage. Individuals strongly, mysteriously affected, are simply semi-entranced, or hypnotically influenced by external spirits, or by an indwelling spirit not their own. The plural, relating to spirits of different grades, may here be applicable. It is reported that out of one of old there went seven demon spirits.

Tutelary divinities, supersensuous influences and conscious spiritual intelligences from angelic altitudes down the scale of being to demons and demoniac obsessions are all about us, and if men as moral agents accept and strenuously appropriate the good and the true, the purer and the higher they transform this life now into an Eden of ecstacy and mortals into the moral likeness of those great seers of old, who like Enoch, walked with God.

Self-contained egotists and railers at things above their comprehension, together with those who sit as officials, figuring for the ingathering of finances, yet never studying nor experimenting with the psychic potencies of sensitives, nor with the hypnotically entranced, nor investigating the marvelous powers of oriental adepts when acting in conjunction with the invisible gods—the above described materialistic worldlings will undoubtedly sneer. No matter! Sneers are not arguments; ridicule is not psychic science, nor are negations and denials so much as an approach to a sound moral philosophy whose foundation is fact and whose bases are experimental study, the higher reason and the testimonies of those dwelling in the super-normal realms of wisdom. Fear constitutes no part of a reformer's belongings. Personally, what I believe, what I know, I dare speak, write, book for posterity. This dispensational crisis calls for heroes; it demands self-sacrificing champions and martyrs. The mob and the moral gibbet are of no account when put in the scales against truth. The betrayal, the denial, the cross, made the Nazarenenan crown that has illumined the ages, all the more glorious.

CHAPTER XIV.

———

"Singularly moved
To love the lovely that are not beloved;
Of all the seasons, I most love winter, and to
    trace
Its eider coverlet of snow,
Nor is in field and garden anything
But, duly looked into, contains serene,
The substance of things hoped for in the
    Spring—
The evidence of Summer not yet seen."

Pre-existence, reincarnation, and a spirit's inhabiting and re-inhabiting another spirit's body for a longer or shorter time for a special purpose, was taught by the Gnostics in the Alexandrian schools and was especially taught by Philo Judaeus, a Greek philosopher of Alexandria living between 20 B. C. and 30 A. D., and who because of his great erudition and eloquence was sent on an embassy to Rome in the reign of Caligula. According to this illustrious philosopher the spirits of mankind do not originate in the world of senses, but come rather from the world of ideas existing in the Divine Logos. They are emanations from God, spirits of His Spirit. They are said by him and other illumined minds to be particles of the verities of the Being who is one with the Logos.

"Of these spirits," states Philo in his work *"De Gigantibus,"* "some descended into bodies whilst others have no desire to come into contact with any part of the earth, but choose rather to remain pure and holy, their only desire being to serve the Father. These are directed by God to watch over and guard mortals; but the first mentioned pursue different paths. Some cast into bodies, as into a stream; are overwhelmed and sink for a time. They pass from sight and sense. Others enter into human bodies for a time. They withstand the pressure of the flesh. They may leave them and enter other bodies not so refined, for the fulfilling of a divine plan, but they emerge from the depths and mount in time back to the source from whence they proceeded. Such souls (spirits) have devoted themselves to wisdom, and from the beginning to the end have striven to throw off the fetters of the bodily existence—or 'die to the flesh'—and so again become partakers in that eternal spiritual life, in the birthless and the imperishable.''

This oriental philosophy so graphically described by Philo, reminds me very forcibly of what has been denominated "the Watseka Wonder." We present a mere skeleton of the case, and as a preliminary, permit me to say that I personally knew this most exemplary family, the Roffs. When delivering some lectures upon foreign travels, in Watseka, I was a guest of this family, noted for respectability, culture and moral integrity; and so, I received the full particulars from the original source. The families concerned were the Roffs and the Vennums. Lurancy Vennum's health was not good. She complained of a queer feeling in her head—of a pressure on the brain, and one day placing her left hand on her breast she fell to the floor in what was supposed to be a cataleptic fit. Her limbs became rigid, as they often are in the early trances

when influenced by the lower, earth-bound intelligences.
The next day the rigid state returned, but her mind
seemed clear after it. 'While in this trance she declared that she saw a number of spirits, describing
them and calling some of them by name, and adding,
"Oh, they are so beautiful!"

A few months later she again became ill with painful paroxysms, muttering strange words (common in
obsessions), then passing after a time into a quiet,
peaceful, unconscious trance. She would claim while
in this supernormal condition to be in Heaven, and
looking earthward could see her body. Not understanding these trances, the allopathic physicians of
the city, and most of the relatives believed her to be
insane and preparations were being made to put her
into the lunatic asylum. At this crisis, Mr. Roff, a
neighbor, believing that this class of spasms and kindred so-called diseases were of a dynamic or spiritual
origin, begged of them not to take their daughter to
an asylum, but to send her to Dr. E. W. Stevens,* a
magnetic physician gifted with great psychic powers.
Reaching the Vennum residence he found 'Rancy, as
they called her, obsessionally entranced, sitting by the
stove, her elbows on her knees, hands under her chin,
eyes wild and staring, and silent. Soon she spoke,
warning the Doctor not to approach, and called the
Vennums bad names. . . . As the friends arose
to depart, she was caught by this untoward occult in-

---

*It has given me great pleasure in the past to know
Dr. Stevens, and a most estimable gentleman he was.
On my return this spring from California through
San Bernardino, I was the guest of one of his rela-
tives.

fluence and thrown violently upon the floor. Dr. Stevens stepped to her side, took one of her hands, as a psychic exorcist would naturally do, and removed the obsessional control—and Lurancy was herself again, with all the grace and sweetness of her real nature. She expressed deep regret that such evil influences approached her unwanted, uninvited. At times she saw them clairvoyantly.

Preparing the way for a higher class of influences, the Doctor asked her (now in her normal state) if she would not like purer and more exalted spirits to control her. "Truly I should," was her reply. "Look about," said Dr. Stevens, "among these many spirits present above and around us, and select someone who will prevent the low, cruel and insane ones from returning to trouble you or the family."

Still clairvoyant, she said: "There are a great number here, the most of them I have never known." Remaining silent for a few moments she continued, "There are many who want to come, yet the angels specify only one that they want to come." Upon being asked who it was she replied, "Mary Roff."

"That is our daughter," exclaimed Mr. Roff; "she has been in Heaven twelve years." He assured 'Rancy that Mary was good, intelligent and when in th body was afflicted much as she was. Afted considering and counseling with the guardian spirits, it was arranged that Mary should enter into and control her body and go to Mr. Roff's home to stay. Mary was delighted with the arrangement. Entering her former home in Rancy's body she was perfectly familiar with everything in the house, recognizing persons that she knew, calling up hundreds of incidents that transpired when in her own body, even the contents of the dresser; but she did not recognize any of the Vennum family. It was a remarkable phenomenon. Think of it! The spirit that constituted the very life and soul of Lurancy Vennum transferred to spirit land and Mary Roff entering, possessing and literally living for fourteen weeks in this body deserted by Lurancy.

Upon asking the incarnated Mary, "Where is Lurancy?" she would reply, "Gone out somewhere;" or "gone to heaven taking lessons . . . and I am here taking lessons and living more closely for a time with my dear ones."

If inquired of where her own physical body was, she would answer: "It is in the ground. I don't want to look at it, nor think of it—that was not I."

She seemed very happy when not thinking or being reminded that she would have in due time to leave the immediate social intimacy with her family friends and return to the higher life.

When Mrs. Alter, her sister, whom she dearly loved, would ask her when, or where she was going, casting her eyes upward for a moment as though listening, she would respond: "The angels tell me I am going to heaven, but I don't know just when." . . . And then she added: "When I got into this body I felt much as I did when here twelve years ago."

Dr. Stevens writes (pages 20-21 "Watseka Wonder"): "Lurancy's body seemed as natural to Mary as though she had been born with it, and yet she could not do with it just as she would like to. She did not seem to realize at first but that this was her own original physical body, until the angels explained it to her, and she had also received information from her parents, sister, brother and friends. So natural did it seem to her after knowing all the facts, that she could hardly feel that it was not her original body born nearly thirty years ago.''

Mary Roff literally lived in Miss Vennum's body for fourteen weeks; and when she returned to the heavenly life she left Lurancy's body in an excellent condition. This was a case all through of wise spirit agency, and the material facts can be substantiated by disinterested witnesses whose veracity was never questioned and whose evidence would settle any case in a court of law.

CHAPTER XV.

MARY REYNOLD'S DUAL LIFE.

"How pure at heart, how sound in head,
    With what divine affection bold,
    Should be the man whose thoughts would hold
An hour's communion with the dead.

"In vain shalt thou, or any call
    The spirits from their golden day,
    Except, like them, thou, too, canst say,
    My spirit is at peace with all."

Another remarkable phenomenon, similar to that
occurring in the Roff family, was that of Mary Reynolds, written out by the Rev. Wm. S. Plummer, and
pronounced a case of "double consciousness"—a
phrase implying little more than self-stultification, and
for the reason that the spirit is *one,* and the consciousness is *one.* The alleged "double" was simply an
accompanying, controlling spirit. Here is the account
summarized from Major Ellicott, Professor of Mathematics at West Point, Dr. Mitchell, of New York, and
others.

Mary Reynolds, daughter of Wm. Reynolds, and
kinsman of Prof. Ellicott, when eighteen years of age
became the subject of what were denominated "fits."
Her general health was poor. One Sunday morning
she was found in the fields, book in hand, and utterly

insensible. Upon recovering consciousness she was
blind and deaf. After a few weeks these senses returned. Three months after this she was found in her
room one morning in a profound sleep from which it
was impossible to arouse her. Her trance, not understood, was intense. After several hours she became
conscious, but was another person. She knew neither
father, mother, nor friends. She had not the slightest
consciousness that she had ever existed as any other
person in the body she was using. She seemed born
into a new world. Everything interested her. She
acquired knowledge rapidly, but her general characteristics appeared abnormal. When her brother,
whom she loved when in her normal condition, came
home from Meadville, she neither knew nor noticed
him. She continued in this state for about five weeks
and then suddenly awoke to her normal state.

These alterations or changes of personality continued for about fifteen or sixteen years, but finally left
her, leaving her at last permanently in the second
state—that is, the original owner and resident of the
body had passed into the higher life, and this "second
state" or controlling spirit had entered her organization, residing there during the remainder of her mortal
career.

Requested by the Rev. Mr. Reynolds to write something of her experience for him and others, she so did,
writing from the standpoint of her "second state," and
relying upon the testimony of her friends for the statements. She says:

"From the spring when the first change occurred
until within eight or ten years, frequently changing
from my first to my second, and from my second to my
first state, I was more than three-fourths of my time in

my second state. There was not any regularity as to the length of time that the one or the other continued. Sometimes I remained several months, sometimes a few weeks, or even days, in my second state. But in no instance did I continue more than twenty days in my first state. The transitions from one to the other always took place in my sleep. In passing from my second to my first state nothing special was noticeable in the character of my sleep. But in passing from my first to my second state my sleep was so profound that no one could awake me, and it not unfrequently continued eighteen or twenty hours.

"Whatever knowledge I acquired in my second state became familiar to me in that state, and I made such proficiency that I became well acquainted with things, and was, in general, as intelligent in that as in my first state.

"My mental sufferings in the near prospect of the transition of either state to the other, but particularly from the first to the second (for commonly I had a presentiment of the change for a short time before it took place), were very great, for I feared that I might never revert so as to know again in this world, as I then knew them, those who were dear to me. My feelings in this respect, were not unlike those of one about to be separated from loved ones by death. During the early stages of my mental disease (abnormality), I had no idea, while in my second state, of employing my time in anything useful. I cared for nothing but to ramble about, and never tired walking through the fields and woods. I ate and slept very little. Sometimes for two and three consecutive days and nights, I would neither eat nor sleep. I would often conceive prejudices, without cause, against my best friends. These feelings, however, began gradually to wear away, and eventually quite disappeared.''

The two lives which Mary Reynolds lived for many years were thus entirely separate. Each was complete in itself, though in reality separated by the portions of the other life intervening. They succeeded each other in uninterrupted succession, as far as the evidence of her own memory or consciousness was concerned. The thoughts and feelings, the joys and sorrows, the likes and dislikes of the one state, did not in any way influence or modify those of the other state. But not only were the two lives entirely separate, but her character and habits in the two states were wholly different. In her first state she was quiet and sedate, sober and pensive, almost to melancholy, with an intellect sound though rather slow in its operations, and apparently singularly destitute of the imaginative faculty. In her second state she was gay and cheerful, extravagantly fond of society, of fun and practical jokes, with a lively fancy and a strong propensity for versification and rhyming. Some of her poetical productions appear to have possessed merit of a high order. The difference in her character in the two states, was manifested in almost every act and habit. Her handwriting in one state differed wholly from that of the other. In her natural state the strange 'double life' which she lead was the cause of much unhappiness. She looked upon it as a severe affliction from the hand of Providence, and dreaded a relapse into the opposite state, fearing that she might never recover from it, so might never again in this life know the friends of her youth, nor her parents, the guardians of her childhood.

These two instances, among others at my command,

present the clearest proofs, being well authenticated, of two different spirits occupying the same body at various times for some purpose not fully revealed in the last case. But concerning these strange phenomena, let none presume to pronounce the word "impossible" unless they have fathomed and tabulated all the laws of nature. Neither should anyone attempt to limit the powers of those mighty spirits above who constitute the hierarchies of the heavens. Denials are as cheap as they are easy. Parrots can assert in very fair English. Telepathy was for a time pronounced "impossible" by the conservative *"unco quid;"* and up to the present the transference of thought or thought vibrations from brain to brain, though a demonstrated fact to the spiritual scientist, is denied or denounced by those who doze in the shadow-lands of biology and psychic phenomena. And so dissociation of the spirit from the body that it has consciously and purposely built up, and its transference into another human body, with the corollary that inferior spirits of varied grades may enter the auras, the blood, the nerve centers and cranial convolutions of others, causing disease and obsession—will be violently opposed by those who have not considered that what is vaguely called space is literally alive with inconceivable numbers of invisible micro-organism, entities and centers of force, among which we daily live and move.

The above stated phenomena will cause:

First—surprise, then a period of disputation, and perhaps acrimonious persecution.

Second—a period of listening, of argument, and of a gradual and general conversion to the newly-taught ideas.

Third—a period when everybody will declare: "Why, we always thought so"—always thought that spirit was immanent in all things—that spirit forces and spirit forms permeate the whole human organism, that spirits detached can enter other bodies and work either good or evil.

Though not a prophet I venture to predict that in less than thirty years it will be difficult to find an intelligent student of psychic phenomena (which includes hypnotism, suggestion, trance, and other spiritual gifts germane to Spiritualism or Theosophy) who will not thoroughly believe, not only in the transference of thought, but in the transference of spirits. I couple Theosophy and Spiritualism together because they are the two sides of one shield— in essence *one,* and that essence consists in lifting multi-millions out of the pit of depressing materialism, and placing their feet upon the rock of spiritual truth.

In further confirmation of spirit detachment—dissociation from the body, and of influencing mortals through the auras, or literally entering into another body, constituting for the time being a distinctly different personality— I submit the following:

In the past I had with me much of the time for fourteen years a superior psychic sensitive. His clairaudience was of a high order, his clairvoyance excellent, and his trances were absolutely unconscious, exhibiting in a marvelous perfection the characteristics of the controlling intelligence. I knew his spirit attendants as well as I did my best mortal-embodied friends. Each was a positive personality, with a different voice, different facial expression, different gestures, and each had a modified different teaching on some matters of the other life. They occupied different spheres or planes of consciousness in the inner-life world.

Conversations with these invisible intelligences were among the happiest hours of these years. When the guides were to put this intermediary into his deepest trance and remove him from his body, save by that etheric cord of sympathy, they would tell me to lock the door, lower the windows at the top, and be self-possessed whatever the marvels might be. When fully in the trance state the whole frame, especially the limbs, would become stiff almost as bars of iron; his breathing would slow down, the pulse in the wrist would cease to beat, and the heart-throb was very feeble. He would lie in this state from three-quarters of an hour to an hour, and returning to his body would relate to me what he had seen. At these times his more ancient teachers accompanied him and guided him while traversing the celestial spaces. He was sometimes overwhelmed with the grandeur and the unspeakable magnificence of the scenery, the temples, the architecture and the white-robed ones that he saw.

During these voyages he met but very few that he knew. He could at any time look back and see his body and those attending to its circulation and respiration. Returning into his body caused a shudder. It seemed to him like dying. Some of the old philosophers compared the original descent of the pre-existent spirit into the human body, to the "darkness of death."

"Why do you believe that this spirit was detached from his material brain on these excursions?" For several reasons!

I. His own positive statements to this effect.

II. The testimony of his spirit attendants, whom I had found truthful.

III. By going off as a spirit to distant cities, seeing and describing what was there transpiring, repeating it to me, and later learning that his description was very correct.

IV. Parting with this sensitive, both going different ways, I have said to him: "Leave your body and come and see me tonight. Remember what you see and report it to me by letter the next morning." This he did, describing many of the minutest things in the room where I slept, and an apartment, too, that I had never been in previously. I never hypnotized this subject, nor could I do so; and weighing all the facts, I insist that no suggestion, no hypnotism, no clairvoyance can account for these facts other than that the Ego left the body and came as a spirit to my room. The phenomenon of a dual personality, a triune personality, etc., is pronounced by an English psychologist "wonderful if true;" but here was a case connected with this sensitive of six or seven personalities; for each of these entrancing spirits claimed to be, and was, a distinct personality and two of them were excessively positive, if not dogmatic, teaching things far above the comprehension of the sensitive and directly opposed to my own opinions. Our controversies upon some of these occult subjects were as sharp as any that I ever had with such personalities—as sectarian preachers in the flesh. One of these controlling personalities when in his earthly body was a French atheist, and he was a rigid atheist still; and to contend, as do some materialists, that these personal entities were "fragments"—were split-off, chip-like, entities from the block (that is, the individualized Ego), exhibits a mental aberration akin to insanity.

Here I am reminded of an able essay by Charles

Dawbarn, of Cal., in a review of Dr. Prince, professor of nervous diseases in the Boston City Hospital, relating to the "dissociation of a personality" and later of several personalities. The Pacific Coast philosopher, Dawbarn, thinks from the spiritual, the real side of things rather than the material, and so naturally furnishes a feast for those who hunger for spiritual truths.

There is a marked distinction between personality and individuality. This must be kept in mind. Miss Beauchamp, Dr. Prince's patient's individuality, was not "broken into fragments." It would be a psychological impossibility. Such a statement is its own refutation. If the Ego, the divine unit, can be broken into "fragments," then farewell to all permanency—there is nothing in a conscious human being that is stable—nothing in this moral universe that is absolutely abiding, but is in a nebulous flux ebbing towards a dreamless nonentity.

Dr. Prince's patient, B., one, was simply a psychological sensitive, and numbers two, three and up to six were individualized spirits occupying different planes of consciousness and conditions of unfoldment. There is nothing strange or marvelous in this case, so learnedly exploited from a materialistic standpoint, to a trained psychologist or cultured Spiritualist. Similar phenomena have been occurring for half a century and more, many of which have been tabulated. The conservatism of stupidity is pitiable, while the refusal of scientists, of physicians in hospitals and of medical doctors in lunatic asylums to thoroughly study hypnotism, mesmerism, trance-clairvoyance, pre-existence and all the recondite laws and finer forces, is almost criminal. When will professional gentlemen in universities and insane asylums, gifted in polysyllabicism, cease confounding personality with individuality, hypnotism with mesmerism, and knowledge with wisdom? In mesmerism, with the touch, there is an emanating aural fluid imparted from the positive to the negative recipient and appreciated whenever there is sympathetic thought and purpose.

Precision in teaching of these occult subjects, suggestion, hypnotism, radio-activity, and psycho-therapeutics, is indispensable to the elucidation of truth. The "Sally" branded as a devil in Dr. Prince's series of personalities was simply a stubborn, positive, undeveloped spirit. This was clearly shown in this 'dissociated' spirit's letter to Dr. Prince: "B, one, is going to be dead (unconscious) all the time to save complications, and because she wants to save you trouble. Isn't she wild? She hasn't made any last will and testament like mine. . . . She ought to make one too, oughtn't she? Some of the spirits who neglected to do so are awfully troubled now, and they try in every way to atone for their carelessness. . . . Do you think B, one, will be a spirit?"

"To me," writes philosopher Dawbarn, "that little extract embodies one of the most important truths in this book, dedicated as it is to science. It is light through a crevice where almost anybody but a cold-blooded scientist would have flung the door wide, and insisted on sharing Sally's knowledge of the world of spirits."

Dissociated personalities, dual and duplex personalities, are spirits disrobed of mortality and connected magnetically with certain mediums; or perhaps abiding temporarily in their aural environments or material organisms. . . . Mme. d'Esperance in her book entitled "Shadowland," treats quite exhaustively of her leaving her body, or witnessing heavenly scenery, and of having the panorama of her own life unrolled before her psychic vision.

CHAPTER XVI.

———

"Ring out old shapes of foul disease,
   Ring out the narrowing lust of gold;
   Ring out the thousand years of old,
Ring in the *thousand years of peace.*

"Ring in the *valiant man* and *free,*
   With larger *heart* and kindlier *hand;*
   Ring out the darkness of the land,
Ring in the *Christ* that *is to be.*"

The following, as germane to pre-existence and a re-return to mortal life, is copied from the "Progressive Thinker."

"I offer my personal experience as an absolute fact—not as supporting any theory. At the time I passed through the experience (28 years ago), I knew absolutely nothing of mediumship in any phase and probably had never heard the word reincarnation. I was then sixteen years of age and had been married one year.

"The knowledge that I was to become a mother had just dawned upon me, when in a vague way I became conscious of the almost constant presence of an invisible personality. I seemed to know intuitively that my invisible companion was a woman, and quite a number of years older than myself. By degrees this presence grew stronger. In the third month after she first made her presence felt, I could receive impressionally long messages from her. She manifested the most solicitous care for my health and general welfare, and as time wore on her voice became audible to me, and I enjoyed many hours of conversation with her. She gave her name and nationality, with many details of her personal history. She seemed anxious that I should know and love her for herself, as she expressed it. She made continual efforts to become visible to me, and towards the last she succeeded. She was then as true a companion to me as if she had been clothed in an embodiment of flesh. I had merely to draw my curtains, shrouding the room in quiet tones, to have the presence manifest, both to sight and hearing.

"Two or three weeks before the birth of my baby she informed me that the real purport of her presence was her intention to enter the new form at its birth, in order to complete an earth-experience that had come to an untimely end. I confess I had but a dim conception of her meaning, and was considerably troubled over the matter.

"On the night before my daughter's birth I saw my companion for the last time. She came to me and said, 'Our time is at hand; be brave and all will be well with us.'

"My daughter came, and in appearance was a perfect miniature of my spirit friend, and totally unlike either family to which she belonged, and the first remark of everyone on seeing her would be, 'Why, she does not look like a baby at all. She looks at least twenty years old.'

"I was greatly surprised some years later when I chanced to find in an old work the history of the woman, whose name and history my spirit-friend claimed as her own in her earth-life, and the fragments of her story, as she had given them to me, were in accord with history, except some personal details not likely to have been known to anyone else. All this experience I kept to myself as a profound secret, for, young as I was, I realized what judgment the world place upon the narrator of such a story.

"Once when my daughter was in her fifteenth year, the first name of my spirit friend happened to be mentioned in her presence. She turned to me quickly with a look of surprise on her face and said, 'Mamma, didn't my papa call me by this name?' (Her father died when she was one year old.) I said, 'No, dear, you were never called by this name.' She replied, 'Well, I surely remember it, and somebody somewhere called me by it.'

"In conclusion I will add that in character my daughter is very much like the historic character of the woman whose spirit said she would inhabit the new form.

"These are my facts. I offer no explanation; if they chance to fit anybody's theory, so much the better for the theory. Theories usually need some facts to prop them up; facts are independent and able to stand on their own feet."

As a well-authenticated case similar to that of Mary Roff and others relating to reincarnation and possession, the following is presented as coming from the spirit spheres through a very superior medium— and is virtually a self-history first published by James Burns, London. *

He said:

---

* (See "Demonism of The Ages and Spirit Obsessions," pp. 225-6-7.)

"A person in any world may climb downward as well as upward. It has been urged by men in the flesh, and by advanced spirits too, that the after state of the spirit is a condition of undeviating progress. Now I deny this. I retrograded in my spirit life; on top of many earthly sins I put a crowning one—I returned to the earth again. I looked backward and inhabited a tenement, and lived in that tenement some four and a half years.

"I stood by the side of the weeping father and mother, over a babe whose spirit was leaving the body. The age or time of its earthly experience was four days; I mean the body had been formed for the reception of a spirit four days. I saw the child's heavenly guide and guardian spirit, and as the spirit of the babe left its house, I saw its guide remove it in its arms, and convey it to spheres in the heavens. I had seen, in my experience on earth, phenomena more wonderful to my philosophic mind than any during my existence out of the body. therefore the wondrous fact to me was a mere fact of conscious individuality out of the body, which led me no nearer to the conception of a Supreme ruling Mind than did the stars which in earth-life I had seen and noticed, and whose motions had been one of my favorite studies—whose immense distances I, with others, had calculated. To sum up, I felt that the fact of the mighty moving masses of matter whirling in space was an infinite, onward, and ever-present fact to me on earth, besides which the mere fact that I was in spirit life faded into insignificance. The one had led me no nearer to God than had the other. I was not religious when inhabiting my earthly body; and I cared little for companionship, when entering the spirit world. I longed for earth's experiences again.

"Unaided by prayer or petition to God, I determined to choose for myself a tabernacle which I could again inhabit and again venture upon earth's scenes, feeling again the passions which had faded but were still held. I determined to find a habitation for my spirit in the body of this new-born babe. In its transition I took advantage of that state in which the spirit of the child was leaving the body, before the mechanism of the physical organization had ceased to act. I succeeded, and in this fragile habitation I, a spirit of a previous sixty-seven years of earth's experiences, took up my abode. My active, restless spirit was perfectly imprisoned in this body. It was ten months ere I could manifest the power of speech through it. I was afraid of crushing the tender fibres of the brain by using them too roughly. At ten months I was able to talk fluently. At two years I could argue with doctors of divinity from the proofs afforded by the Hebrew writings of the prophecies respecting the coming of the Messiah. At four years I was able to talk fluently English through this body, and some four thousand Latin words. At that age I entered into studies with the greatest anatomists living. I was then enabled to meet in argument the most noted divines, ignoring the authenticity of Bible records. I was too anxious to bring my talent forward in its habitation; my architectural studies, my mathematical exercises, performed at the age of four years and four months, were the wonder of all the leading minds. Fluently I could answer all questions in history. Passionately fond of mathematical studies until the brain formation collapsed—broke—understand me perfectly, because I am incapable of conveying my ideas to the outside world, as through this glass (taking a tumbler off the table)

would be incapable of holding water were I to control
the arm holding it and dash it on the floor. The en-
velope was no longer fit to contain the spirit; I aband-
oned it, having had for four years and nine months a
second earth-life—a veritable reincarnation.

"Occupying this self-chosen habitation but four
years and nine months with immense difficulty and
through incompetency when, for the first time, dawned
the fact—there must be a God."

The doctrine of reincarnation held by so many millions, has under its various forms the substratum of
truth. Spirit is ever reincarnating into, infilling, molding and imparting life to matter. Each living person
is a distinctive proof of a series of reincarnations.
Physiologists inform us that the softer parts of the
material body change in from three or four months to
a year. When the finger-nail is removed by the surgeon's knife, in sixteen weeks a new one appears; and
the whole body is not only changing, but in every seven
years it has been completely thrown off through the ex-
cretions, as a mask, or as chaff is thrown off from the
ripened wheat. Personally, then, I have been reincarnated fully twelve times; that is, I have had twelve
different human bodies, the individual, or conscious
Ego, remaining the same only with an increased power
of manifestation.

In the spirited discussion upon reincarnation between the lamented Dr. Helen Densmore, New York,
and myself, I made the following statements in the
last pages of that book:

"A spirit disrobed of gross materiality, dwelling
in those Elysian realms afar, incarnated temporarily
for a purpose when it descends into the atmosphere of
our earth and vestures itself in such atoms, ions, and

refined etheric elements as it can manipulate and polarize for the accomplishment of some grand achievement.

"The psychic emanations, the etheric envelopes of an individual extend outward from one to to five to some twenty feet, depending upon the will and potency of the personality. And these radiations in their color reveal the character. Now then, when a spirit descends from some higher, brighter zone of immortality into the radius of this human aura, it really reincarnates to impress and inspire for some praiseworthy end. This is rational. That the flesh-dismantled Ego, purposely freed from the etheric soul-body, may reincarnate for some good purpose, is plausible and reasonable. This was doubtless true of Krishna, Jesus and Gautama Buddha.

"Again, an illustrious spirit intelligence, seer or sage, afire with love and beneficence, looking upon this world of struggle, competition and crime, may earnestly desire to enlighten and uplift humanity onto a higher spiritual plane; accordingly, in the sacred impregnating moment of the pre-existing spirit implantation, he projects a magnetic thrill, a thought-ray of light into the sensitive life-germ. This magnetic, molding ray, substantial to the spirit eye, purposely willed and psychically perpetuated by this heavenly benefactor, be he musician, mathematician, artist or poet, energizes and measurably molds the fetus, the infant, the child—the heaven-impressed, spirit-incarnated child—which is often pronounced 'a great genius.' Here, then, is the golden key, that unlocking, rationally explains reincarnation—rationally without puerility, speculation, or the extravagant theory that every human being is chained—*fated* to pass through,

Sisyphus-like, 'every possible experience of this world,' (many of which would be brutally degrading) before reaching the beatific spheres of blessedness. Such a dogma, whether pagan or Christian, theosophical or spiritual, is preposterous and shocking to the mind of either seer or laurel-crowned sage.

Under the husk the corn is found; and so under much loose verbiage and extravagant imagery pertaining to oriental lands is found the truth of reincarnation—the entrance of the Ego into human bodies, which when lifted from the limitations unwisely thrust upon it, shines a brilliant star in the constellation of spiritual regeneration and the higher righteousness.

11

CHAPTER XVII.

———

"Beloved, I wish above all things thou
Mayest prosper and be in health, even as thy soul
　　prospereth."

　　　　　　　　　　　　　　　　—John.

"I have heard of a mystic organ, which God's own
　　hand has sealed:
Not a single note from its silent keys through the
　　dim years has pealed.
The hands of angels are searching to waken the strains
　　sublime
Shall make glad tidings re-echo through the corridors
　　of time."

These are the last days of May, and nature is
dressed in her best. She has forgotten her wintry wind-
ing-sheet of white, and now smiles through a leafy.
maze of foliage. The clouds gathering in the blue roll
in majestic grandeur through the sky. The rains fall,
and the resistless rivers run seaward bearing their
burdens of deposit and drift—and these—all these are
effects, and effects pre-suppose pre-existing causes.
Moving objects visible to the eye imply a propelling
force or forces, which forces and motions are but via-
ducts. They are not original causes. Whatever potency
there may be in them comes from somewhere else.
They are not self-contained causes. Rivers do not
grow, only as fountains flow into and feed them. Certainly, the impulse to feed on high trees, preceded the

giraff's long neck. The musician precedes the music
that peals out from the organ. Matter did not come
into the brain by thinking, for there was neither brain
nor human beings when this earth was a seething mass
of red-hot fiery fluid. Thought implies a thinker, and
cannot owe its origin to anything mechanical in structure. The unity of nature and the fixed order manifest,
even to the coming of an eclipse, indicates an intelligent
purpose and omnipotent power. This power, exclaimed
the inspired John, is "Love." "God is Love"—and
that love extends high as the highest heavens, deep as
the lowest depths, and embraces in its all-encircling
arms of sympathy, the intelligences of this and of all
worlds. Here is faith, confidence and sweet rest to the
troubled spirit.

Religion, a deep, spiritual emotion, like every other
law of life, repeats itself—moves in cycles, inversely
from circles in incarnations to angles and crosses and
from these back to the spiral circle, spirally climbing
round and round in infinite progression, the lapses
being parts of the whole—ripples that startle,
then blend with the river of time. The child that falls
grows stronger by the struggles to rise. Every step
that the prodigal son took away from the luxuries of
his father's house was spiritually one step, through
the experiences of husks and poverty and bleeding
feet, nearer to the father's home of changeless love.

The Ego is pure. The inmost spirit does not sin.
Vices come through the angularities and the imperfec-
tions of the soul-body, which though etheric is particled
and out of harmony with the pulsations of the enthroned spirit. And so all are imperfect, because dwelling in and functioning on this material plane of being;
and all, likewise, are artists, painting on invisible can-

vas; all are sculptors, chiseling on invisible marble; all are writers, writing books in the invisible ether. All have their ideals—lofty ideals unattained.

Nature is a unity. History proceeds in regular cycles. There are transitional points but no broken links—no aimless causes. The dew leaves its effect upon the plant. The dashing stream writes its history on the mountain-side, the fossil in the rock.

Though possibly not germane at this point, nevertheless the inspired words from the higher spirit life upon this subject of the spirit's pathway, are appropriate. It will be remembered that Rev. John Pierpont, a poet-priest, was for years one of the brightest, bravest men in the ranks of Unitarians, and who when becoming a Spiritualist had the moral and manly manliness to say it straight out in the humble home and the denominational pulpit, and who still speaks thrilling words of inspiration through the trance-attuned lips of Mrs. M. T. Longley, Washington, D. C. In his lecture appearing in the *Progressive Thinker,* Spirit Pierpont says: "God, Nature, Intelligence; call it what you will, is working in its own beautiful way—is doing this work, sending out the soul-flame into the universe from its Central Source of Light. . . . Thus do we claim that we are a part of the Supreme; thus do we claim we are called to live in the living presence of the omnipotent power; thus do we claim we have the right to call ourselves children of the living God, for it is true that from that great central source cometh every flame of light—every soul that finds expression here or elsewhere in the vast universe. . . . This soul-germ appears like a *point of brilliant light* in the midst of this magnetic substance which it has for its support;

that it is in form somewhat like a small fig, and
by and by this substance increases; instead of
decreasing it gathers to itself new elements from
the atmosphere and this increases its size, but it
retains the same shape, and after a time it comes
to look something like a beautiful pear, only it
is still of a white, vapory appearance and substance
and power, until by and by, following the law of
attraction, just as surely as all things in life must
follow that same omnipotent law, this soul-germ is
swept into the atmosphere along the currents of expression of some human being upon this mortal plane;
in this magnetic environment or aura it becomes absorbed, and then will come the processes of gestation
and of growth in a material sense. The soul becomes
absorbed by this co-ordination of forces that is creating a mortal form, and when the life principles—the
positive and negative elements—are blended together,
this soul-germ, seeking expression through these outly-
ing forms, comes into active conscious life on earth.
The conditions of earth may be such—and also those
of heredity—through the material processes of life, as
to cloud this soul power; as to in a measure cramp
and gather around it that which we may call a shell or
sheath. It may seem to be for the time crystallized so
that it can not give out this scintillating radiating
power which makes for good; but all the while the
soul is there—it can not possibly be destroyed—it
knows no fear. The soul itself is of the Infinite; it
cannot be lost whatever its conditions or lack of growth.
. . . Such is the life of the soul, as far as we can follow
it into the mortal state; but the life of the soul, we
might say, has only just begun, provided that the soul-
germ comes fresh from the infinite life to the mortal

state of earth. It may have passed through various forms of expression in other worlds, on other planets; we do not know.

"There are those which have, and which do not come in that soul-germ or form of which we speak; but we are confining our description to the soul-germ we have reason to suppose has had no previous expression through any form of activity and consciousness yet pre-existing in the bosom of Infinite life."

Whether this poet-preacher's verses were ever collected from journals and magazines and booked, I do not know. They should have been; and so should the beautiful poems of that sweet-souled and noble minded Unitarian Spiritualist, William Brunton. Here are snatches from the poet Pierpont's religious gems:

"I tread where the twelve in their wayfaring trod;
I stand where they stood with the chosen of God,
Where His blessings were heard and His lessons were
      taught,
Where the blind were restored and the healing was
      wrought.

"Oh, here, with his flock, the sad Wanderer came!
These hills he toiled over in grief are the same;
The founts where he drank by the wayside still flow,
And the same airs are blowing which breathed on his
      brow."

Treating of travels in dark barbarian lands, where neither science nor a rational religion was known, he wrote, let

"A lonelier, lovelier path be mine;
Greece and her charms I'd leave for Palestine;
There purer streams through happier valleys flow,

And sweeter flowers on holier mountains blow;
I'd love to breathe where Gilead sheds her balm,
I'd love to walk on Jordan's banks of palm,
I'd love to wet my feet in Hermon's dews,
I'd love the promptings of Isaiah's muse;
In Carmel's holy grots I'd court repose
And deck my mossy couch with Sharon's blooming
    rose.''

Traveling much in oriental climes, looking as I did
upon the rocky isle of Samos that gave birth to Pythagoras, who taught both pre-existence and social com-
munism; standing upon the spot where Socrates was
imprisoned for denying the gods and corrupting the
young—I can well understand why from extensive
reading the poet Taylor wrote, using Emma Rood
Tuttle's words:

''A poet sang to a thrilling harp
    Of the island of Long Ago;
And the angels hearkened, and mortals wept,
    O'er the music's refluent flow;
Both spirits and mortals held their breath,
    The song was so sweet and low.''

Yes, that Isle of the ''Long Ago'' takes many of us
with whitened hairs far back along the winding dusty
trail to a father's toil in the field, and a sainted mother's
kiss by the hearth-stone—to the sunny days and
sports of childhood—to the crystal brook by the hill-
side where sported the speckled trout—to the grim and
grimed old school house by the roadside—to the fairy
dreams in early youth of crowns and castles—to joyous
hopes that withered and died and were buried in their
budding—to the silent churchyard that we used to shy
when the night-winds sighed through the willows under

which the forms of our loved ones slept and over which
the grassy turf had been wet with our tears—to the
dear old fruit-laden orchard, the red and white roses
by the door-way, the sweet scented honey-suckles that
shaded the windows, and the old "moss-covered bucket
that hung in the well." Blessed, yet fading memories
of the long ago—fading, and yet they hauntingly cling
to us as does the "scent of the roses" to the broken
vase.

Serious, if not sad, while contemplating the Isle of
the "Long Ago," Mrs. Tuttle, inspirationally catching
the strain, sings to us as naturally, as encouragingly,
of that lovelier Island of the by and by. The angel of
optimism overshadows her—she thus sings in part, of
the golden future. Listen!

O poet! singing your soul away,
    Your song is a sweet-breathed sigh;
But turn about while the finale flows
    From your fingers, and cast your eye
Adown Time's stream; there's an island there,—
    The island of By and By,

.   .   .   .

It is sweet to know, that, as one land fades,
    The other is growing near.

The Long Ago is the realm of forms
    Bitterly, bitterly dead;
The hand is ice with the broken ring,
    Marble the sacred head.
The harp is mist with the broken string,
    Gone is the voice which led.

The Long Ago is a burial-place,
    Marked by its marbles cold,
The bells which rock in the steeples gray

Are ever solemnly tolled;
There Joy hangs off like a distant star,
But Ruin and Change are bold.

But By and By is the realm of souls,
The region of fadeless blooms;
Upon the rim of its vernal shores
Never a breaker booms;
And never a storm-cloud in the sky,
Pitted with darkness, looms.

When the clouds lift up and the wind is fair,
Look out with your soul, and see
The silvery foliage wave and flash
High up in the sapphire sea:
Each leaflet speaking as 'twere a tongue,
"Here is *immortality.*"

Aye, thrice blessed truth—"Here is immortality"
—here in Spiritualism is the clear, irrefragible demonstration of a future, conscious existence.

It has been remarked that every man is born either a Platonist or an Aristotelian; otherwise, he has a mental drift in the direction of one or the other of these illustrious Sages. It was one of Emerson's sayings that some men have the "Orient in their constitutions." This meant that they had an affinity for the dreamy occultism of the East. It is surely attractive to the calm, meditative mind. The pessimistic Schopenhauer was Asiatic in his philosophic sympthies. Kant was purely European. Emerson was an American with an outreach into the cosmopolitan and the universal.

The philosophy of Unitarianism, Theosophy and Spiritualism are in essence one. They constitute a right-angle triangle of which Spirit—Divine Spirit, is the base. Thus constituted, they as naturally as logically infuse higher and more hopeful principles into materialism and those tottering forms of sectarianism that tend to cramp and crush the noblest aspirations of human nature. The pulsing potency of Spiritualism centers in spirit—the spirit of life and light and love, and would be infinitely more palatable to the multitude without the *ism* attachment. The march of the world's progress has been impeded by the mastery of isms. They bode no good. They build partition walls between man and his brother man, and disintegrate rather than unite and harmonize.

Spirit, in the fellowship of love, is the great, the mighty word of the Twentieth Century, because it over-arches, underlies, infills, unifies, and spiritually uplifts. It draws no lines of caste—knows no sacredotalism--seeks the good along every pathway—stands for the unprejudiced investigations of all subjects, all forms of thought, all genuine phenomena, all human experiences, and accepts all truths that can be verified. Eminently eclectic, it excludes, condemns, no one, realizing that the most beautiful painting has a shaded background—that the minor chords help to swell and intensify the melody; and that from the darkest prairie soils the finest corn springs up and ripens under autumn's sun.

"The universe is but a thought expressed
    And through the thought a strange, sweet music
    A grand, sweet strain to every heart addressed;
    A strain divine for every soul that weeps.

"The silver sheen that lines the robe of night
    Foretells the life that past the shadow lies;
Aurora's gleam and evening's rays but write
    God's love upon a page of summer skies."

There is in the universe no absolute retrogradation—no eternal annihilation. Such a destiny would be directly opposed to the love of God and to those axiomatic principles which show that things existing with the same thing, coexist with one another; and that whatever is true of a whole class, is true of whatever belongs to and is brought under the class; and the class, the series, the races of human beings, come under the class, the law—the law of evolution—which in its mighty, majestic sweep, lifts all conscious human intelligences through methods diverse and often mysterious, upward and onward, through the eternities—one grand purpose, one divine law, one purposeful life, one heartfelt fraternity, and one final destiny, and that spiritual unfoldment, ever becoming, ever aspiring, yet never reaching absolute perfection and infinite power.

Thought—the higher thought—looks up hopefully to the ideal; science hews the pathway towards it, and the religion of brotherhood beckons, urges the wayfarer on the way—all helpers.

By far the ablest journal in the country devoted to the dissemination of that teaching known as New Thought, is *Mind;* and the editor in a recent issue as justly as logically said: "The term New Thought is in a way a misnomer. There is nothing intrinsically new about the view of life so designated, though it is new to many people." This in him was true and manly.

Its vitality lies in spirit, which is life itself. Another writer in this journal remarks: "The glory of the New Thought consists in the fact that it insists on the psychological law, operating through ideal suggestion in all religions and in all ages. By ideal suggestion I lift myself into communion with the most Godlike creatures (angels and spirits) that I can conceive of. By the same power I heal my body of physical ailments,' etc., all of which is only an exhibition of the higher Spiritualism, Spirit being the foundation and the pillars that rise in such majestic proportions.

Spirit, the sweet spirit of fellowship and love, does not antagonize, does not condemn, but interpenetrating, softens, soothes and tenderly lifts the suffering soul up onto the highlands of trust and rest. It is not the rough winds that remove the dry leaves which autumn's frosts and winter's snows have glued to the trees, but the warm suns of springtime touch the dead leaves and they fall that the new buds and green leaves and sweet blossoms may come out to beautify field and forest. There is infinite variety in nature and also in the expressions of truth. Non-essentials have their places. Meditations and kindly controversies upon pre-existence, reincarnation, reputed communications from Mars and other planets, tend to stimulate thought and elicit new conceptions of life and destiny, all of which broaden the horizon of research and widen the panorama of investigation, furnishing records to be deposited in national archives, and so handed down to posterity. Monotony tires while diversity inspires and illumines the student of nature. The various instruments in a great orchestra have their uses in evolving richest melody, but they must necessarily be tuned to a uniform pitch, else harmony would be impossible. Diversity in unity is the voice of nature—and opportunity the inalienable right of all.

The spirit of Spiritualism not only levels to the same dust prince and peasant, but levels all human pride and all abnormal distinctions of race. It heals all internal obsessions, wards off external obsessional influences, and throws a subtle magnetic network around all those who strive and struggle in sincerity for the good, the true, and the morally pure. These "are mine anointed," says the Angel of Redemption. "Touch them not."

On a line of marble pillars fronting Herod's Temple off from the Court of the Gentiles, was inscribed in Greek and Latin—"No foreigner may go further under penalty of death." It is hard to think—to know that the Herodian era of selfish exclusiveness has not utterly perished. Theological walls and ecclesiastical fences separate those who profess to follow Him who, weeping by the grave of Lazarus, had "not where to lay His head." The cold, grim walls around the residences of millionaires remind us of medieval times when houses were forts and the windows port-holes for shooting down strangers. The spirit knows no strangers, no foreigner too far off not to arouse sympathy in the hour of suffering.

> "Thy brother! 'Tis the suffering man
> Though at the farthest pole."

Thank the gods! No mercenary millionaire, no society caste can wall out God's sunshine, fence away the cooling showers, hush the whispering breezes, still the music of the forest birds, nor bottle up the delightful odors of the multi-million flowers that make fragrant the airs of morning and evening-time. There are sunrise and sunset pictures that no great brown fronts can hide, and hearts so warm and friendship so unselfish and souls so brimming with the fires of love that no floods can quench, nor length of years blot from the memory. God is good. His tender mercies are over all his works, and this is a beautiful world—

a world where every winter has its spring, every briar bush its berries, and every pang of pain its hidden recompense to be realized, if not to-morrow then in some sunny incoming future.

That sweet-natured spiritually-minded English author James Macbeth Bain, tells in his books when treating of the Christ-spirit of love, that "man as a spirit can talk with his soul." He can admonish it to patience. He can control his emotions by saying—"Be still, my soul." In these words he recognizes the three-fold nature of man, ratioed as body, soul, spirit. He further writes: "I would sing of the cross. I would chant the joys of abundant suffering. I declare the blessedness of manifold tribulation." And the Patmos visionist, under a similar wave of inspiration, saw that the whitest robes and the brightest crowns were worn by those who had "come up through tribulations deep."

It is related by the historians of the first century that John lived to be over one hundred years of age, and that they held in profound reverence this aged and living saint, who sorrowed with Christ in the garden, stood by him at the cross, received in charge the mother of Jesus and clairvoyantly beheld his freed spirit ascend to the homes of the angels. And when he had become too old and weak and infirm to walk to that little primitive church-edifice in Ephesus, his admiring brethren would take him in their arms and carry him thither, his presence being a very baptism. Feeble in body, yet strong in the spirit, he would rise at the close of the service, and in a trembling voice could only say: "Little children, love ye one another." Departing from the services to their humble homes, they would say among themselves, the tears falling—"Behold how he loves us—behold how our sainted brother loves us.

It was he who said, *God is Love*—let us love one another.''

This English writer afore referred to, author of ''The Brotherhood of Healers,'' further says: ''Through sorrows, through manifold experiences, wonderful in their kind, but sore to the flesh and hard for the natural soul to endure, thou hast gently led me, and I can say, standing in the eternal light, no longer do I seek fame or worldly esteem. There is nothing of earth that I desire. But the young soul within me yearneth strongly for the good and blessedness of the poor and despised and forlorn and weary ones of the world's estate who are as pilgrims on this earth.''

''Divine is the Christ, beautiful the angels of love! Behold the enlightened mind is still the storehouse of the good things of the Eternal, and the eye of the soul can even now be opened to receive glimpses of the wondrous beauty of the land of the Spirit, to see beyond the shadowy forms of our every-day surroundings into the mysteries of the state that really is, and passeth not away.

''Truly, it is good for us to realize that at the end of our journey through this shadowland of trial and many sorrows, there remaineth, for all who would enter in, a new country of Life the blessed, from whose face the beauty, the peace, and the gladness never pass away, where, as the most enlightened of our saints of Scotland sings:—

'The red rose of Sharon unfolds her fragrant bloom.'

And that rose is the substance, of which our earthly one, howsoever fair it be, is only the shadow.''*

The emotion of prayer just now overshadows me. ''Pray without ceasing'' was the apostolic command. Pray standing or kneeling, pray in garden or grove, pray by the bubbling fountain in the forest, pray in your spirit's silence, pray, for prayer is an output towards the good for humanity, and an uplift towards guardian angels and good spirits. Prayers, thanksgiving and invocations must not be used interchangeably. They are not spiritual equivalents. We thank God, invoke the angels, and pray to the good spirits. It is right to pray for the dead, and beautiful in them, the so-called dead, to pray for us. Every kind, outbreathed thought is a prayer. Every smile of love that causes a smile to play upon the face of sorrow is a prayer.

Let us pray!

O Thou Infinite and Eternal Spirit, the consciousness and the life of the universe—Thou whose loving presence is manifest in all things from the sands upon the seashore to the stars that blaze in the heavens, we thank Thee—thank Thee as our loving, unchanging Father—Mother. True, we cannot comprehend Thee. Neither can the babe comprehend the mother's love or the father's hand that leads. Our spirits look up

---

* His books:—

''The Song of The Cross,''
''Breathings of the Angel's Love,''
''The Bitter Herbs of Cleansing,''
''The Opening of The Gates,''
''The Selfless Love,'' etc.

To be had from all London booksellers, and ought to be from American booksellers also.

in gratitude to the ideal unattained, to the rock from whence we were hewn, to that fountain of infinite love and wisdom, feeling, trusting that all is well—all is well. And while we thank Thee, Thou Life of all lives, we pray to the angels of God in the sweet trusting spirit of the Christ, for help and guidance. Recognizing all races and nationalities as our brothers, we cry for light—more light. We are seeking to know the truth in its purity and fulness that we may live thereby. Extinguish in us all remains of vain ambition—fill us with the Christ-spirit of Charity—pervade us with universal love—make us humble and teachable as children, and give us more abundantly of the wisdom of the angels. O ye hierarchies of the Heavens that delight to do the Father's will, send thine angels to quicken our spiritual natures—inspiring us to forgive and to go about like the Master of old, doing good, and help us, O help us to help others—to bless others that we may be blessed; and may we so live that when the last mortal hour draws nigh we may see the sweet faces of our friends and hear their voices—"Well done, ye good and faithful ones of earth. Come to your homes celestial, where tears never fall nor suns of progress never set. Amen.

Knowledge, inspired by love, and guided by wisdom, constitutes the twentieth century ark of safety—soul brotherhood! Spiritualism, the great wisdom truth of the ages, gives knowledge for the sectarist's impotent and tremulous belief in a future existence. The demonstrations of a present spirit communion are positive, innumerable, overwhelming, and absolutely undeniable; and further, they reveal the tremendous fact that consciences are the soul's accusers, and that justice and mercy follow rational beings in all worlds,

12

as do the days and nights. This is a universe of order. God reigns, and ultimately, in ways oft mysterious to us, the good triumphs, transforming the thorns that pierce into white roses, which blooming, send their fragrance down through the intermingling races into the far-off ages. . . .

Though now an octogenarian and more, by five years, life was never so sweet and golden. I look back over the long journey, trying and tangle-footed at times, without a sigh or a tear; nor do I say pessimistically, 'it might have been.' God and his ministering angels ever know best.

"Once I sorrowed that the golden day was dead,
Its light no more the countryside adorning;
But whilst I grieved, behold! the East grew red
With morning.

"Once I sighed that merry spring was forced to go,
And doff the wreath that did so well become her,
But, whilst I murmured at her absence, lo!
'Twas summer.

"Half broken-hearted I bewailed the end
Of friendships than which none had once seemed
nearer,
But, whilst I wept, I found a newer friend,
And dearer.

"And thus I learned old pleasures are estranged
Only that something better may be given,
Until at last we find this earth exchanged
For heaven."

Having once had the honor of meeting Victor Hugo in a Spiritual seance in Paris, Mrs. Hollis Billings being the sensitive, I feel to use these words of his:

"I feel in myself the future life. I am like a forest once cut down; the new shoots are stronger and livelier than ever. I am rising, I know, towards the sky. The sunshine is on my head. The earth gives me its generous sap, but heaven lights me with the reflection of unknown worlds. You say the soul is nothing but the resultant of the bodily powers. Why, then, is my soul more luminous when my bodily powers begin to fail? Winter is on my head, but eternal spring is in my heart. I breathe at this hour the fragrance of the lilacs, the violets, and the roses, as at twenty years. The nearer I approach the end the plainer I hear around me the immortal symphonies of the worlds which invite me. It is marvelous, yet simple. It is a fairy tale, and it is history. For a half century I have been writing my thoughts in prose and in verse; history, philosophy, drama, romance, tradition, satire, ode, and song, I have tried all. But I feel I have not said the thousandth part of what is in me. When I go down to the grave I can say, like many others, 'I have finished my day's work.' But I cannot say, 'I have finished my life.' My day's work will begin again the next morning. The tomb is not a blind alley; it is a thoroughfare. It closes on the twilight, it opens with the dawn.''

Consciousness is cognate with existence itself. When spirits from these mortal lands meet those gone before, instantly, by sympathy, they recognize each other. Pure love is immortal, and unselfish friendships eternal. A beautiful guardian angel once said to her earthly mate: "Mind echoes to mind; heart throbs with heart. Together we will read heavenly beauties; together sing one melody of love; together twine garlands to deck the brows of sorrowing mortals; together tread eternal pathways and bathe in life's

fountain of light. We shall be there together; no sickness, no deaths, no partings. I am ever near thee. Ask
me not to come. Shall the rose say, ' I wait for fragrance?' Does it invite sweetness? Thus are we
united!"

"I shall know her there! I shall know her there,
  By the shining folds of her wavy hair,
  By her faultless form, with its airy grace
  That an angel's pen might fail to trace—
  By the holy smile her lips will wear,
  When we meet above, I shall know her there!

"I shall know her there, and her calm, dark eyes
  Will look in mine with glad surprise,
  When my bark, wild-tossed o'er life's rough main,
  The far-off port of heaven shall gain;
  Though an angel's robe and a crown she wear
  By the song she sings, I shall know her there!"

Death is nature's process of laying down a fleshly
burden, and the rising of the spiritual into the brightness and beatitudes of immortality. Burning is pre-
ferable to burying the forsaken tenement. Mourning
garments, useless and often expensive, are but sombre
mementoes of the dark ages. Black, with its aural
emanations, is repellent to the lovely home-imagery of
angelic life. The dying often smile, but never weep.
Put flowers on the door knob, and garland the cold
form with lillies and wreaths of rose-buds.

Personally, I feel as though I had but just begun
to live—to see, to comprehend. Heights rise above me,
and I am conscious of the mighty immensities lying
beyond. I long to go—and yet;—

"If I can live
  To make some pale face brighter, and to give
    A second lustre to some tear-dimmed eye,
Or e'en impart
  One throb of comfort to an aching heart,
    Or cheer some wayworn soul in passing by;

"If I can lend
  A strong hand to the fallen, or defend
    The right against a single envious strain,
My life, though bare
  Perhaps of much that seemeth dear and fair
    To us on earth, will not have been in vain.

"The purest joy,
  Most near to heaven, far from earth's alloy,
    Is bidding clouds give way to sun and shine,
And 'twill be well
  If on that day of days the angels tell
    Of me: 'He did his best for one of Thine.' "

PART II.

"Great is the might of Truth, against whom shall be arrayed the intelligence, the cunning, the ingenuity of man, the well-laid plots of the whole world, yet she will with ease defend herself."—Cicero. Pro Caelio, XXVI, 63.

Increasing years with their multiplied observations and experiences convince me that a great majority of the controversies afloat in journals, magazines and books of a dogmatic character, arise from the imperfect definitions of words and proper understanding of the terms employed. Take the word soul as a sample. The lines of this hymn are sung in all Christian lands:

> "A charge to keep I have,
> A God to glorify;
> A never-dying soul to save,
> And fit it for the sky."

And so we have persistent reiterations from platform and pulpit—"a never-dying soul," "a precious soul to save," "God have mercy on my soul," "man's immortal soul," etc.; and yet not one of these phrases occur in the Hebrew or Christian Scriptures, in the extensive works of Philo, the Alexandrian Jew who flourished from 30 to 50 B. C., or in the classic authors. They often used the word soul, but not in the strict sense of an endless existence.

Proclus, the Neo-Platonic philosopher, in treating of the energizing Presence of the Universe, said in substance—"God is Causation;" and Jesus uttered these memorable words, *"Pneuma Ho Theos"*—Spirit is God.

What thought can be mightier or more uplifting than that this Spirit, essential, immanent, immutable and omnipotent, is God, and that we as conscious, rational beings, are made—evolved, if you choose the word—in the "image of God." Thinking back to the Hebrew period we read that the "Spirit (ruach) of God moved upon the face of the waters." Be sure the word *ruach* (Hebrew) is sometimes rendered mind, breath, wind, etc., but it would be a most awkward translation to say that "God breathed wind (a gentle zephyr) into man and he became a living soul." Ruach and Neshamah are both used in the Old Testament. Here is an example (Job. XXVI-4): "To whom hast thou uttered words? and whose spirit (Neshamah) came from thee?" In Proverbs we read: "The spirit (Neshamah) of man is the candle of the Lord." Rationally interpreted, God "breathed," by the law of influx, vibration into man, a potentialized portion of himself, and he became truly a son of God. All human beings are sons of God manifest in the flesh— all human beings are spirits now; and an inspired biblical writer exclaims: "Then shall the dust return to the earth as it was, and the spirit (*ruach*) shall return unto God who gave it."

The general use of *Pneuma,* is spirit, with its correspondents in the classical writings, in the Septuagent, in the Apocrypha, Philo, Josephus, the New Testament, and especially by Paul, who in very plain language, wrote to the Thessalonians: "I pray God that your whole spirit and soul and body be preserved blameless,'' etc. Here the distinction made between soul and spirit is very definite. And again this Gentile apostle speaks of the ''dividing asunder of soul and spirit as with a two-edged sword.''

It is reported by an eminent Greek scholar that Æschylus used the word *Pneuma* (spirit) five times, Euripides 112 times, Thucydides 11 times, Zenophon 11 times, Plato 5 times, Aristotle 124 times. In these well-marked cases they were speaking of the divine breath, the spirit, the real, indivisible inmost of man. But when treating of mind, courage, life—they generally used a different word—*Psuche.* Hence Jesus asked: ''What shall it profit a man if he gain the whole world and lose his own soul (Psuche)?'' Life.

Philo, composing his voluminous works during the first half of the first century, used the word *Pneuma* 116 times; and in the estimation of this most illustrious scholar, the human spirit was an emination—a radiating portion of the divine spirit—the Ego, ''which God breathed into man as a ray from his own blessed and thrice happy nature.'' (De Concup II.)

It is safe to say that the most eminent linguists and philosophers of the present, as well as those illustrious sages who have long summered in the heavens, differentiated soul and spirit, the latter word relating more directly to immortality. The Scriptures speak of the ''destruction of both soul and body in Hades,'' but the destruction—the death—of the spirit, is never spoken of by any of the ancient or modern literati. Quite as well speak of the death of the *Infinite,* for God is Spirit, essential, absolute and immutable.

The phrase ''immortal soul'' we repeat, does not occur in the ancient Hebrew or Christian Scriptures.

Philo Judaeus, the learned Alexandrian Jew, living from 30 to 50 B. C., used the word spirit about forty-seven times in his earliest writings, and always as allied to life, or immortality, or God, "Who," he declares, "breathed the Spirit—mark, the *Spirit*—into man."

Soul (Nephesh in the Hebrew) has been a sort of a verbal vehicle for many ambiguous ideas. In biblical language souls are born and souls die.

The "ruach" (Hebrew), "pneuma" (Greek)—spirit—is not an accumulation of aggregates—not a bundle of thoughts, emotions and warring attitudes; but is noncomposite, uncompounded and indestructible—an entity, an involutional influx from God, the One—the All—Who alone hath underived immortality.

The Greek philosophers, though in different phraseology from biblical writers, propounded the same rational truth. Hence, the Roman Marcus Aurelius, while urging that life was a unit—that the sensations were subjective—taught also that the "soul (the soul-body) was a refined, corporeal organism."

Auberlin, a Tubingen graduate and Basel professor of theology, states that "the spirit is the spiritual nature of man as directed upward, and is capable of a living intercommunion with God, while the soul is the diffused, quickening power of the body, as in animals, and, pertaining to, is excitable through the senses."

Porter, on "The Human Intellect," declares that the word "soul" differs from "spirit" as the species from the genus; souls being limited to a spirit that either is or has been connected with a body or material organization, while a spirit may be applied to a being which has not at present, or is believed to never to have had, such physical connection.

Delitzsch, in his Biblical Psychology, assures us that the "Psychical functions of the soul are types of the spiritual functions, the broken rays of their colors. But the soul is no Ego. It is to be distinguished from the spirit. The inner self-consciousness, which forms the background of the spirit-copied functions, is that of the spirit, and is related to the Infinite Spirit from which it had its origin."

When Samson (Judges 15-19) was supposed to be dead, "when he had drunk water his spirit returned to him again."

So, when the Egyptian was found dying, or dead, from hunger and thirst, they gave him bread and water and "his spirit came to him."

"The spirit of man is the candle of the Lord." Prov. XX-27.

"Then shall the dust return to the dust as it was, and the spirit shall return unto God Who gave it." (Eccles. XII-7.)

"In Whose hand is the soul of every animal, and the spirit of all flesh that is human." Here is a marked contrast between the soul and the spirit.

The book of Baruch mentions both good and "evil spirits (demons) who work mischief;" and Peter, with an eye probably upon the book of Tobit speaks of the spirits in prisons to whom Jesus went and preached the gospel. And Paul, in writing to the Hebrews, refers to "the spirits of just men made perfect." Here we have the striking contrast, "spirits" in the "City of the living God," and imprisoned spirits in Hades

(Hell) to which Jesus ministered—but all were spirits —not souls, nor immortal souls.

And Jesus said, "Maid, arise," and her spirit came again and she arose straightway."

In the agony of death Jesus cried out, "Father, into Thy hands I commend my spirit."

And when the first martyr, Stephen, fell, his cry was, "Lord Jesus, receive my spirit."

And now, with all this array of testimony, Jewish, Grecian, Neo-Platonic and philosophic from philosophers, together with our present-day entranced intermediaries speaking of their spirits, their Egos, leaving their bodies, etc., there are uncultured mortals and unfleshed intelligences entrancing sensitives who will deliberately persist in using the word "soul"—"the immortal soul"—in the place of spirit. They ought to know better—ought to do better. The soul, the soul-body, or the etheric intermediate (of the same form as the material body), is particled and changeable. It may be dissolved and die, but the spirit—the larger, higher, diviner self—the *spirit*—never! It is God within us.

While the word soul covers in a measure the personality of man, the word spirit, pre-existing, covers to the fullest extent both the personality and the individuality of man, and must never be thought of as an abstraction, but rather as that divine energy—that conscious reality—which permeating, molds the structureless into the structural, and transmutes composite rarified substances into forms. This reality, the spirit in activity, constructs, builds up the soul-body that it dwells in, and when sufficiently perfected can detach itself from the psychical body by the will and travel in the cosmic regions of space. And even if not highly developed, advanced scientific spirits can aid the spirit to temporarily leave the soul-body for the educational experiences of witnessing and studying the scenery of the higher life. This detached spirit, when afar distant from the earth-plane, often meeting, recognizes other spirits and it may be seen by independent clairvoyants occupying a similar plane of spiritual unfoldment.

Spiritualism, dismantled of frauds, superstitions and bigotry, is the greatest, the divinest word of the century, and is so because it centers in God, Who is Spirit, immanent, immutable, omnipresent. Let this thought sink deep into your heart. God is Spirit, man is a spiritual being, and spirituality is the highest life to live. "Know you not," wrote the inspired apostle, "that you are the temple of God, and that the spirit of God dwelleth in you. The temple of God is holy, which you are." This "temple of God," said the Patmos visionist, "is four square," corresponding to the physical, mental, moral and spiritual make-up of man —and broadening the panoramic vision, it corresponds to the four great religious, Brahminism, Buddhism, Christianity and Mohammedanism, with their almost numberless branches and isms, which when summed up, the number of their wars, conquests and crimsoned sins in the name of religion—summed up, numbered, tabulated and named, mean *Babylon!* "And I heard a voice out of Heaven," said the apocalyptic visionist, saying, "Babylon is fallen! Behold, Babylon is fallen. . . . And there shall be a new heaven and a new earth. . . . The tabernacle of God is with men and He will dwell with them and they shall be His people, and God Himself shall be with them. . . . And God shall wipe away all tears from their eyes, and there shall be no more death, neither sorrow nor crying, neither shall there be any more pain, for the former things are passed away.''

When this glad era comes! To many it has already come. These understand the ''mystery of the seven stars.'' They have ''overcome'' and received ''the white stone,'' and their names are known in the ''new heaven.''

Yes—the glad era of which poets have sung and prophets have prophesied, is coming. It is at our doors. These convulsions in nature—these political struggles and degenerations—these mad rushings for gold, and pelf and power—these religious controversies and pronounced heresies, are the evidences. The sword of justice is unsheathed. The ''right shall rule,'' is the voice that comes from heaven, and the echoing reflex of this voice jostles the crowns of kings and emperors, winnows the chaff from the wheat, and speaks from the skies in thunder tones—*''The right— the right shall rule.''* As of old:

> ''Men saw but thorns on Jesus' brow,
> But prophets saw the roses.''

When that good time comes—and now so near—it will be seen that these religious cults with their divisions and sub-divisions, were but preludes and prophecies of the inauguration of that one great religion— that one universal religion, whose basic foundation will be spirit—one God and one humanity. Its cathedral will be the universe, and its temple, for square, will be consciousness, love, wisdom and brotherhood.

Invisible psychic influences, termed obsessions, whether by elementals, spiritual degenerates, floating entities, or wandering vitalized centers of force, relate themselves to and interpermeate the rarefied elements and essences of the soul-body, but not the non-composite Ego, the pure spirit, linked to the Infinite Spirit —God. And this will remind the reader of the following passage in the "Demonism of the Ages and Spirit Obsessions, pages 198-254, and others.*

"It must be considered that all obsessions are not from unseen surrounding intelligences. There is a sort of an ideation obsession caused by an unbalanced, weakened organization giving place to acting internal forces. Everything subjective and objective affects these persons. They are like tremulous aspens. They are partly the victims of their own disordered imaginations. They are emotional, suspicious, pessimistic sensationalists, touching the fringe-belt of morbidity, hearing the unheard, and seeing fanciful pictorial presentations instead of genuine realities. This sort of obsession is remedied by auto-suggestion and mesmeric manipulations scientifically administered."

. . . "Sickness may be caused by transmitted tendencies, climatic conditions, ignorance, and violation of

---

* It gives me pleasure to state that Dr. G. Lester Lane, 872 Huntington avenue, Boston Mass., a cultured gentleman, influenced according to conditions from three planes of spirit life, the mental, the spiritual and the celestial, has almost miraculous success in demagnetizing, relieving, and curing the obsessed. Blessings and commendations are the results of his work in this direction. There are others also who have the gift of exorcism.

natural laws; hence is not always caused, as certain extremists have taught, by thought—by thought trans-ference and hypnotic suggestions, etc.''

. . . "There are internal entities, internal monads and internal acting emotions antipathetic to man, which obsessing, weigh down and deplete, vampire-like, disor-dering and injuring the finer elements of the sensitive soul-body, the effects of which manifest in the physical body, known generally as chronic diseases—epilepsy and nervo-inharmonies.''

Allowing physiologically and anatomically seven years to perfect a complete change from cells to sin-ews, and from sinews to bones in the human body, I am now in my twelfth reincarnation, and through them I have rigidly retained my individuality, but not my personality. That was the subject of flux, ebb and flow, according to circumstances and environments. Each incarnation measurably affected the succeeding. And yet, no one should be judged and tortured for the frailties of a former incarnation. None are perfect. Each admitting the truth of evolution and unfoldment should be judged, if judged at all, for just what they are to-day. To twit, as did a low-browed New England parson, John B. Gough of intemperance when in his middle and mature years, and thrilling multitudes with his telling temperance orations, was considered so base and morally villainous that the New England press scathingly condemned this pretentious parson who assumed the prerogative of detective, prosecutor and judge.

Among the good words unspoken and spoken at present is the word "now"—*The Now*. This thought was neatly expressed by that poet, Universalist and Spiritualist, Alice Carey in these lines:

"I said if I might go back again
  To the very hour and place of my birth,
Might have my life whatever I chose,
  And live it in any part of the earth;

"Put perfect sunshine into my sky,
  Banish the shadows of sorrow and doubt;
Have all of my happiness multiplied,
  And all of my suffering stricken out;

"If I could have known in the years now gone
  The best that a mortal comes to know:
Could have had whatever will make man blest,
  Or whatever he thinks will make him so;

"Yea; I said if a miracle such as this
  Could be wrought for me at my bidding,—still
I would chose to have my past as it is,
  And to let my future come as it will.

"I would not make the path I have trod
  More pleasant or even more straight or wide;
Nor change my course the breadth of a hair
  This way or that to either side.

"My past is mine, and I take it all,—
  Its weakness, its folly if you please;
Nay, even my sins, if you come to that,
  May have been my helps,—not hindrances.

"So let my past stand just as it stands,
  And let me now, as I may, grow old;
I am what I am, and my life for me
  Is the *best*—or, it had not been—I hold."

And the same line of inspired thought is beautifully expressed by Abbey Walker Gould of Moline, Ill.
She thus sings in flowing rhyme:

"When in a time of darkness there is wrought
  Upon a seed, some careless hand let fall,

The mystery of a life undreamed, unsought,
   And strange imaginings woven over all.
When mist and sun and summer cloud,
   Have each in turn served out the purpose sent,
There will come back reward unthought
   Of forces, which unto that seed was lent.

"Souls are the seed, sent down to earth,
   From out the Paradise of God,
They touch each other from their birth,
   Until they skyward leave the clod!
Whate'er of sweetness, or of love,
   That to the soul shall fragrance bring,
Will come three-fold its worth to prove
   And in their heart a love-song sing."

It is needless to say that every individual is enveloped in a personal atmosphere of his own. To this
fact, the N-Ray is in evidence; and this surrounding
N-Ray encasement reflects every one's real moral
status, and these aural emanations, which now so
clearly reveal character to the clairvoyant eye, inter-
blend with the auras and vibrations of multitudes of
unfleshed beings, the majority of whom are temporarily
tethered to this earth-plane of existence. So tethered,
their teachings are none the more authoritative because
they are invisible. Theories are as varied in the Tar-
tarean sphere of the after life as they are in this fric-
tional world of thought and theory. This thought led
Mr. Myres to suggest in his great book that "there are
alien and hostile intelligences beyond the shadows of
death;" and so are there good spirits, angels and arch-
angels beyond these shadows, and their powers for
good are increasing. The star of progress is in the
ascendent in this and in all worlds; and touching the
great hereafter it will be considered and said sooner

or later, as friend after friend departs—''Gone—gone in appearance only, to join

''The choir invisible
Of those immortal dead who live again
In minds made better by their presence.''

In the meantime, remember that when you are speaking or writing of a future eternal existence, to use *spirit* instead of the word soul, for souls grow, souls change, souls may disintegrate, souls may die, their soul-substances returning back to the realm from which they originated; but spirit, God incarnate in man, is immortal, because rooted and grounded in God—the invisible, the immortal, the omnipotent *ONE*—the All.

A LIST OF OUR MORE IMPORTANT
BOOKS AND PAMPHLETS

A LIST OF OUR MORE IMPORTANT BOOKS AND PAMPHLETS.

"Thinking and reading," said the English Dr. Johnson, "make the wise man."

Those who have read the Hindu "Book of the Pitris" (spirits) the Hindu "Institutes of Manu," or witnessed Hindu evocations to their ancestral gods, or their Shraddha at and after funerals, need not be told that the Hindus believe—*know*— of spirit intercourse and obsession.

The Chinese have been called by English and American residents in that far-off country, "an Empire of Spiritualists." Their mediumship was witnessed by Dr. Dunn and myself in the streets of Hong-kong and Canton, China. Japan spirit-converse is almost universal. The Koreans practise it in some form from the lowest up to the royal family. The Utah mormons and our Indian tribes of the northwest are rigid believers in a converse with the spirits of the dead. And millions of Americans today believe in and know such converse to be a fact. Only materialists of the Haeckel school pronounce it impossible.

The eminent naturalist and scientist, Alfred R. Wallace, published these words a while since:

"My position, therefore, is that the phenomena of Spiritualism in their entirety do not require further ·confirmation. They are proven quite as well as any facts are proven in other sciences."

And the distinguished writer upon psychic and psychological subjects, Thomson J. Hudson, says in his "Law of Psychic Phenomena," (p. 206):

"The man who denies the phenomena of Spiritualism is not entitled to be called a skeptic; he is simply ignorant; and it would be a hopeless task to attempt to enlighten him."

[198]

1—THREE JOURNEYS AROUND THE WORLD.

A large, handsomely bound octavo volume, 500 pages, finely illustrated, describing the Pacific Islands, New Zealand and Australia, India and her magic, Egypt and her pyramids, Persia, Ceylon, Palestine, etc., with the religious manners, customs, laws and habits of foreign countries. Price, $1.25 (reduced from $2.00). Postage, 10 cents.

2—IMMORTALITY—THE OCCUPATIONS OF SPIRITS.

What a hundred spirits say about their dwelling places, their locomotion, their social relations; infants, idiots, suicides, etc. Price reduced from $1.50 to $1.00. Postage, 12 cents. Paper, 50 cents. Postage, 12 cents

3—SEERS OF THE AGES.

This large volume of 400 pages (9th edition) treats exhaustively of the seers, sages, prophets and inspired men of the past, with records of their visions, trances and intercourse with the spirit world. This is considered a standard work, treating of God, heaven, hell, faith, repentance, prayer, baptism, judgment, demoniac spirits, etc. Price reduced from $2.00 to $1.00. Postage, 15 cents.

4—SPIRITUAL HARP.

A book of 300 pages, containing songs, hymns and anthems for Spiritualist societies and circles. The words are afire with progress. It contains the choicest songs and music by James G. Clark and other reformers. Reduced from $2.00 to $1.25. Postage, 10 cents.

5—THE CHRIST QUESTION SETTLED.

A sharp symposium by Hudson Tuttle, W. E. Coleman, Rabbi Wise, Colonel Ingersoll, J. S.

Loveland, B. B. Hill, J. R. Buchanan and Dr. Peebles. This is a handsome volume of nearly 400 pages, and treats of Jesus, Mohammed and the agnostics. What the Talmud says about Jesus. 6— Antiquity unveiled. Colonel Ingersoll's agnosticism. What the spirits through W. J. Colville, J. J. Morse, Mrs. Longley, Mrs. Everitt, Mrs. Hagan-Jackson Brown and other mediums say about Jesus, etc. Price reduced from $2.00 to $1.25. Postage, 15 cents.

7—THREE JUBILEE LECTURES.

A most elegantly bound pamphlet of 122 pages, giving Dr. Peebles' lectures delivered in Hydesville, March 31, 1898, in Rochester, and later in London at the International Congress of Spiritualists. These lectures, illustrated, are racy, and scholarly. Price, 20 cents. Postage, 3 cents.

8—REINCARNATION—(Hear All Sides).

Considered and discussed *pro* and *con* by Dr. Densmore, W. J. Colville and Dr. Peebles, the latter stoutly denying the truth of this old *"Hindu-borrowed theory."* It contains over 100 pages and is neatly bound. Price, 30 cents. Postage, 5 cents.

9—THE EIGHTIETH BIRTHDAY ANNIVERSARY OF DR. PEEBLES.

This is a handsome pamphlet of 50 pages, containing an account of the birthday reception given Dr. Peebles when eighty years old, in Melbourne, Australia. Poems from friends in many parts of the world were read, speeches made by the Australian leaders in Spiritualism, and a characteristic speech by Dr. Peebles in reply. *"How to Live, to Live a Century."* Price, 15 cents. Postage 2 cents.

10—DEATH DEFEATED, OR THE PSYCHIC SECRET OF HOW TO KEEP YOUNG.

This book goes to the foundation of things—health, the foods to eat, the subject of marriage, the causes of divorce, animal, flesh-eating, what Herodotus, Hesiod, Homer, Pythagoras, Shelley, Graham and others ate, the foods that produce long life, and how to live "immortal" on earth, etc. Very handsomely bound in cloth. Price, $1.00. Postage, 15 cents.

11—VACCINATION A CURSE AND A MENACE TO PERSONAL LIBERTY.

This finely illustrated volume of between three hundred and four hundred pages, treats of inoculation, cow-pox and calf-lymph vaccination from Jenner's time to the present. It tells how the cow-pox pus poison is obtained—how the vaccine virus, while causing many deaths, sows the seeds of eczema, pimpled faces, cancers, tumors, ulcers and leprosy. It gives a history of the several years' battle against vaccination in England, Parliament making it "optional" instead of compulsory. This book should be in every school library and family. Price, $1.00. Postage, 12 cents.

12—SPIRITUALISM VERSUS MATERIALISM.

A series of seven essays printed on cream-colored paper, elegantly bound in cloth and is pronounced one of the ablest of the Doctor's works. These essays were written at the request of the agnostic, H. L. Green, editor of the *Free Thought Magazine*. Price 40 cents. Postage, 5 cents.

13—A NEW BIOGRAPHY OF J. M. PEEBLES, M. D., BY PROFESSOR E. WHIPPLE.

A magnificently bound book of 600 pages, giving

a complete account of the life of this *"old pilgrim,"* and indefatigable worker in reform for 65 years. The Doctor has been actively engaged in the Spiritualistic field for over fifty-five years, being a convert while it was yet in its infancy. Consequently this book contains quite a complete history of Modern Spiritualism. It is intensely interesting, and marvelously cheap for a book containing so many personal facts and precious truths. Price, $1.00. Postage, 16 cents.

14—SPIRITUALISM COMMANDED OF GOD.

This pamphlet deals especially with Spiritualism as opposed to orthodox churchianity, and especially the Seventh-Day Adventists. The arguments are pointed and biblical, and such as to completely silence the churchianic objections to Spiritualism. Price, 15 cents. Postage, 2 cents.

15—THE ORTHODOX HELL AND INFANT DAMNATION.

This is one of Dr. Peebles' most scathing writings upon sectarian doctrines, creeds and preaching. His quotations from orthodox sermons are reliable and authoritative. This large pamphlet is especially recommended to those seeking knowledge on this the great blunder of orthodoxy. Price, 10 cents. Postage, 2 cents.

16—SPIRITUALISM IN ALL LANDS AND TIMES.

A pamphlet of 31 pages treating of the Spiritualism of Zeno, Socrates, Homer, Hesiod, Plato, Plutarch, Cicero, Jesus, the early church fathers, the Quakers, Shakers, and the advanced minds of all past times. Price, 10 cents. Postage, 2 cents.

17—THE FIRST EPISTLE OF DR. PEEBLES TO THE SEVENTH-DAY ADVENTISTS.

This is one of our latest pamphlets, being a scorching reply to the many attacks of the Seventh-Day Adventists. It is argumentative and to the point, in a sharp, clear-cut style. Price, five cents. Postage, 1 cent.

18—A PLEA FOR JUSTICE TO MEDIUMS.

A pamphlet dealing with mediumship, giving valuable advice to sitters and investigators concerning the proper conditions necessary to high-class manifestations. Price, five cents. Postage, 1 cent.

19—PRO AND CON OF SPIRITUALISM.

This bound pamphlet of 25 pages is a reprint of those stirring essays in which Rev. H. A. Hart endeavored to prove "Spiritualism dangerous" and allied to "witchcraft." Conceding to many requests, the Doctor has put his replies in pamphlet form to insure a wider circulation. Price, 10 cents a copy. Postage, 2 cents.

20—FIFTIETH ANNIVERSARY OF MODERN SPIRITUALISM.

An elegant pamphlet containing an account of the exercises at Rochester and Hydesville, N. Y., at the celebration of the fiftieth anniversary of modern Spiritualism. It contains the addresses of the most noted speakers present, with illustrations of the Fox girls' home. This pamphlet makes a very pretty memento to Spiritualistic literature. Price, 10 cents. Postage, 3 cents.

21—DEMONISM OF THE AGES AND SPIRIT
OBSESSIONS.

This great work contains XXXIII chapters—as follows:

I. Evil Spirits—and their hypnotic influences.

II. Chinese Spiritism—A Demon in the Kwo Family.

III. Responses to the Nevius Circular Concerning the Works of Evil Spirits.

IV. More Demoniac Possessions in China— Responses to Circular of Inquiry.

V. Demoniac Possession in Japan and Korea.

VI. Demoniacal Obsessions and Possessions in India—Clairvoyance.

VII. More Stubborn Facts Concerning Demoniacal Possessions in Oriental Lands.

VIII. More Testimonies to Hindu Demonism.

IX. The Demonism of the Ancient Greeks, and the Australian Aborigines.

X. Judean Obsessions and the Actions of Demons in Jesus' Time.

XI. New Testament Demonism and Unclean Spirits, "cast out."

XII. The Haunting Places of Demons.

XIII. Evil Spirit Obsessions Afar, and Near in Our Seance Rooms.

XIV. Pitiful Letters from the Obsessed and Possessed.

XV. More Letters from Spiritualist Mediums Relating to Obsessions.

XVI. Obsessions of the Early Methodists and Others.

XVII. Obsessions Caused by Liquors and Gambling Dens.

XVIII. Obsessions and the Assumed or False Names of Spirits.

22—THE SPIRIT'S PATHWAY TRACED.

This manuscript-book, now in press (the revised proof being read), is a volume of between 200 and 300 pages, and will be ready for its readers on or before the 1st of September. It treats of the beginning of things, of the nature of the human spirit. Did this spirit pre-exist—when did it enter the mortal body—What is its form—How does it relate to the soul-body? Can it leave the human form and return into it again? Can it live in and control another mortal body? Is the spirit an aggregate of qualities or an imperishable unit, etc., etc. Price, 75 cents. Postage, 12 cents.

23—WHAT IS PRAYER?
DOES IT AFFECT GOD?

A valuable pamphlet on the abuses of prayer, the nature, efficacy, and value of true prayer. (Ready for the press.) Price, 15 cents.

24—IS THE DOCTRINE OF "WHATEVER IS, IS RIGHT," TRUE?

A sharp review of some spiritists, Theosophists, and mental scientists' positions who teach that "All is Mind," "All is Right," "All is Good," "All is Lovely," "Whatever is, is Right." (Ready for the press.) Price, 15 cents.

25—ARE ANIMALS IMMORTAL?
DO THEY EXIST IN THE SPIRITUAL WORLD?

This pamphlet will help to settle the ever-recurring question whether insects and animals are to be found in the spiritual world. The discrepancies of spirit-teachings, and the positions of A. J. Davis, Cora L. V. Richmond, Hudson Tuttle, and others, are quoted. (Ready for the press.) Price, 20 cents.

INCORRECT—UNTRUE.

It has been said that Spiritualists are not readers of Spiritualistic literature; that they prefer excit-

[206]

ing stories and trashy novels. *I consider this charge untrue.*

Spiritualists generally read, it seems to me, what is readable and really instructive.

It has been further said that they "Manifest no interest in such missionary work as distributing Spiritualist books, pamphlets and leaflets as do sectarists, Theosophists, and Christian Scientists." *This I think also is measurably incorrect.*

These books and pamphlets may be obtained of Dr. J. M. Peebles, Battle Creek, Michigan, 70 North Ave.; J. R. Francis, 40 Loomis St., Chicago; and Spiritualist and liberalist booksellers generally.

CPSIA information can be obtained
at www.ICGtesting.com
Printed in the USA
BVOW06s0837130217
476036BV00016B/244/P